N315B

Michael Tomkinson
NORWAY

with text by Alf R. Bjercke

First published 1991 by
Michael Tomkinson Publishing,
POB. 215, Oxford OX2 0NR
Second (corrected) edition 1993
Reprinted 1995

© Michael Tomkinson 1991, 1995

Designed by Roger Davies
and Michael Tomkinson

Printed by CS Graphics Pte Ltd.
in Singapore: ISBN 0 905500 46 6

Contents

Publisher's preface

Norway is a country to which, where history and ecology are concerned, we other Western Europeans should perhaps feel apologetic. At school we were taught of the Vikings, a destructive Nordic horde that sailed persistently to Anglo-Saxon England to raze, rape and pillage with enviable vigour. They were the very incarnation of the Dark Ages, a negation of whatever civilization there then was.

This historical fixed image was the work of the Vikings' foes and victims. When Norsemen in the late 8th and early 9th centuries first turned their attention to England (and Ireland), their obvious objectives were monasteries and churches – poorly defended but well endowed with valuables entrusted by absent notables and legacies given in exchange for paradise. As monks and clerics wrote most contemporary records, the Vikings (like the Vandals in North Africa) do not fare well in written history. The far from impartial image perpetuated by dispossessed churchmen survived the Reformation and, despite Richard Wagner's attempts to romanticize it, stuck. A thousand years after vanishing from history, the Vikings are still tarred with the early Church's brush.

Kviteberg Farm and the Kvænatindene mountains

Scientific research tells a very different story. The Vikings, excavations show, not only raided but traded and settled in well-ordered communities. Jorvik (York) was by AD 950 the largest Viking town; even Dublin exceeded in size any settlement in the Norsemen's homeland. At Jorvik, as Alf R. Bjercke writes, 'there was not a single weapon among the 17,000 items found'. Artefacts discovered there and on other Norse sites reveal the Vikings to have been the foremost craftsmen of their age. Kenneth Clark's *Civilisation* has as its very first illustration the prow of a Viking ship.

The clergy's concern for chastity would also have made Norse morals anathema. Untroubled by this minority's Judaic-Christian inhibitions, the feminine sector of the public by and large was no doubt less dismissive of the Vikings' advances. Fear of the *furor Normanorum* may have been fomented from the pulpit, but the peoples of Britain and north-western Europe were steadily permeated by fair means as well as foul. The older family-names of England, Scotland and Ireland owe their Fitz- and Mac- prefixes to Viking founding fathers. Norsemen enlisted or were conscripted into the 'Great Army' that the Danes imposed on England. The English monarchy for some 300 years was intimately interlinked with Norway's. Modern findings make it advisable to keep an open mind, perhaps even be in two minds about the Vikings.

It is not only Norway's forebears but also its present-day forests and fisheries that suffer unjustly. Pollution from industrial neighbours is an increasing problem. Effluent from Britain's industrial north ends up here as acid rain; smoke from factories contributes, as in Britain and Germany, to *Waldsterben*, dying forests.

The amount of sulphur precipitated on Norway by acid rain between 1979 and 1987 is reckoned by ecologists to be some 1,835,000 tons. Acid rain has emptied most lakes in southern Norway of their fish; to counteract acidity, those in the east of the country are being frantically treated with lime. The higher the altitude, the lower the acidity level lethal to freshwater fish. While those in mountain lakes succumb at levels which fish at lower altitudes survive, the latter still die of malnutrition when acidity eliminates the organisms they feed on.

It is precisely twenty years since Norway first brought this unneighbourly conduct to the notice of a British cabinet minister. Despite representations, delegations and parliamentary missions, the last two decades have seen only aggravation.

All this, a disingenuous author might suggest, is reason to hasten a visit to Norway. Pollution, though, until it is halted, will affect only specific aspects of environment and wildlife. Generally, it can make little mark on the rugged grandeur of a land unchanged since the last Ice Age. For Norway's reputation with visitors from overseas rests less on shipping-fleets, fisheries or off-shore oil; foreign aid, diplomacy or its intermittent history; on Laplanders, reindeer, goat's cheese, moose or the midnight sun, as on its natural beauty: snow-capped peaks, glaciers, rivers and lakes; the uncounted islands that fleck a formidable coast; the fjords that wind, Wagnerian, between sheer cliffs, and attractive-awesome waterfalls.

The names Norwegians give these features are often quite as awesome. Hoarily unpronounceable to the first-time visitor, Norway's place-names sometimes appear disconcertingly long (although Norwegian is basically a brisk, terse language that befits a practical, sea-and-mountain people not given to Byzantine circumlocutions or meandering romanesques). Or their blunt monosyllables – Ål, Gol, Hol and Hell – might be thought better suited to a lesson in phonetics than a place. If meaning anything at all, they necessitate a dictionary, or an obliging native to translate.

Most polysyllabic place-names owe their length to the Nordic and Germanic device of merging two or more words into one. Honey (*Honning*) Bay (*Våg*) thus becomes Honningsvåg; the North Cape is Nordkapp, and Vestvågøy 'West Bay Island' (*øy*).

Many place-names can also be made more manageable by discounting the final -*en* or -*a*. The Norwegian definite article, these suffixes are used with most natural features: the map's *Oslofjorden* is thus (the) Oslo Fjord; *Magerøya* '(the) Meager Island', and *Bergsdalen* '(the) Mountain Valley' (or 'Dale').

Remembering these, and the very few terms below, will help those with no knowledge of Norwegian to appreciate place-names that, although perhaps tongue-twisters, are often descriptive or even poetic. In town: *gate* 'street' (pronounced like garter), and the compass points *Nord* (pronounced 'nor'), *Sør* (as in Sir), *Øst* and *Vest*. Inland: *fjell/fjellene*, 'mountain/mountains', *tindene* 'peaks' and *vidda* 'steppe' or 'moorland'. On the coast: the above-mentioned *ø/øy/øya*, *våg* and fjord (plural *fjordene* – pronounced 'fjorene' in most Norwegian dialects); *vik* 'inlet', *sund* 'sound' (of sea), and *nes* 'point' or 'cape' viz. a topographical 'nose'.

Arctic Circle sign on Hestmannøy,
'Horseman Island': 66° 33' N

Geography. Norway is – as its old Norse name of *Nordvegr* (the Northern Way) suggests – the most northerly country of Europe. At 71° 10′ 21″ N, the stark bleak Nordkapp/North Cape on Magerøya is considered to be the northernmost tip of Europe, the nearby Kinnarodden the most northerly point of the European mainland. A lesser superlative is Norway's westernmost position in the geographical and political bloc which, with Sweden and Denmark, comprises Scandinavia.

Relatively narrow from east to west (at its widest 270 miles, at its narrowest, near Narvik, only four), Norway broadens from north to south. Like a fractured tadpole it drops, head down, from an arctic latitude further north than most of Alaska to southernmost Lindesnes at 58° N. The north-south distance is, as the crow flies, some 1100 miles but creeks, bays and fjords convolute the coast-line to a length of over 13,000 miles. Off-shore rocks, reefs, skerries and some 150,000 islands complicate navigation but protect the coastal settlements from the full brunt of the North Sea. The land area measures officially 125,064 square miles which, with a population of 4·2 million, means in theory almost twenty acres of space for every man, woman and child.

To the north, west and south, Norway is bordered by water: first the Arctic Ocean, then the Norwegian and North seas, and finally the Skagerrak that reaches south to Denmark. Inland, the mountains called Kjølen (the Keel) form the eastern boundary with Sweden: from the frontier bridge at Svinesund all the way up to the Three Countries Monument in the province of Troms. Here Finland becomes Norway's neighbour for 400 miles of uninhabited heath and mountain terrain, as far as the next Three Countries Monument in the upper Pasvik Valley of East Finnmark. From here to the Jakobselv border at the mouth of the Varangerfjord, about 112 miles, Norway has since 1945 neighboured Russia.

If, until glasnost, this north-eastern frontier played its part in the Cold War, the literal warmth of its north-western areas gives Norway a unique distinction. Nowhere else in the world does human habitation extend so far north – as far as the 71st parallel, in fact, all of 4½ degrees inside the Arctic Circle. That Norway remains arable and habitable so far north is due to the Gulf Stream, the North Atlantic Drift. The same warm transatlantic current that (usually) makes Britain's winters less severe continues its flow, and its tempering effect, along the Norwegian coast.

Administratively, the country is divided into nineteen *fylker*, usually translated as provinces. Each *fylke* consists of from one (in the case of the capital) to 44 *kommuner*. The capital, formerly Christiania, was in 1925 renamed Oslo. The population is increasing at 2·9% per annum and, with it, the popularity of the hereditary monarch, Harald V (who succeeded to the throne on the death of his father, the much–loved Olav V, on 17 January 1991).

Geology. Where a country's attractions are largely geological, some account, albeit simplified, is warranted as to their origins. Norway has not always been the 'Land of the fjords and mountains' that we know. Aeons ago, it was flatter and low-lying – more Netherlands than Nordic – with much of its land-area then beneath the ocean.

The folding of the Caledonian mountain chain occurred some 400 million years ago and, in three mountain-forming episodes, shaped the backbone of Scandinavia, continuing northward via Spitsbergen and Greenland to Newfoundland and the eastern part of North America. (The geology of eastern Canada, in particular, corresponds very closely

5

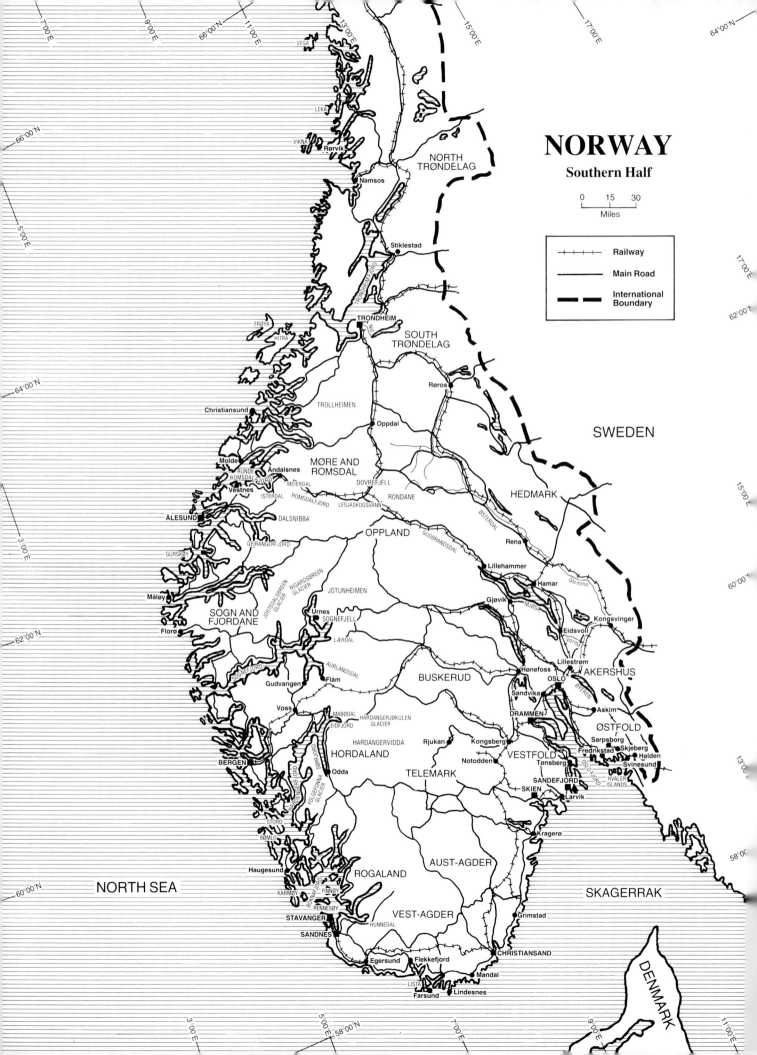

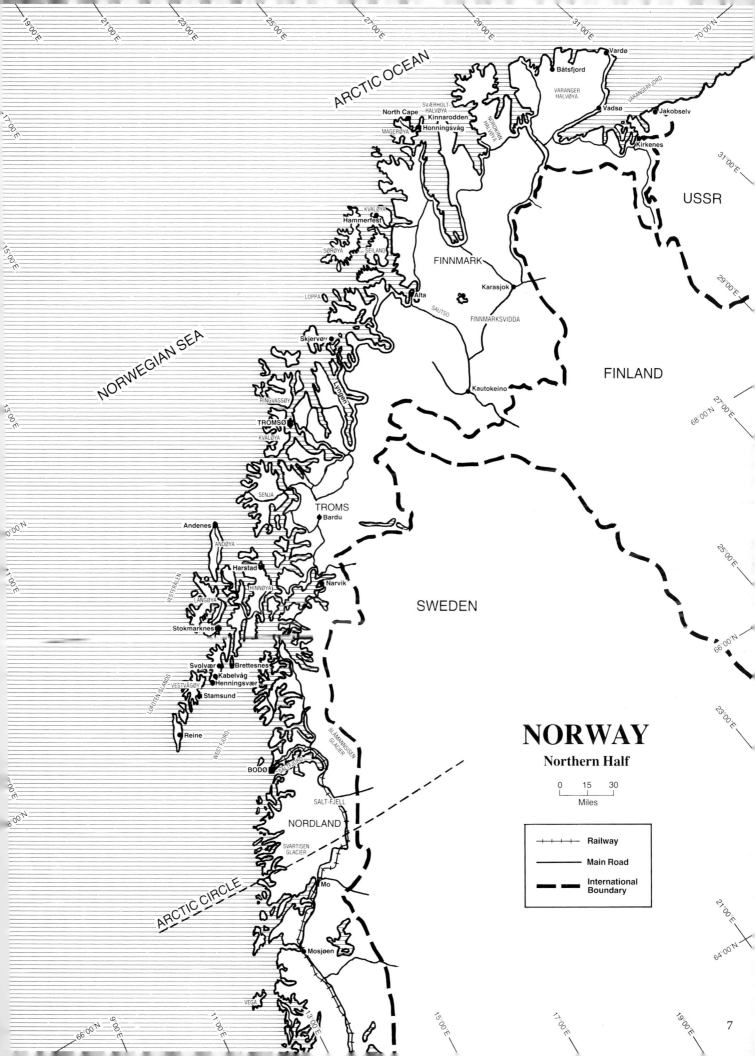

ARCTIC OCEAN

Vardø

Båtsfjord

VARANGER
HALVØYA

North Cape
SVÆRHOLT-
HALVØYA
Kinnarodden
Honningsvåg
MAGERØYA

NORDKINN
HALVØYA

Vadsø

Jakobselv

VARANGERFJORD

Kirkenes

KVALØYA

Hammerfest

SØRØYA

SEILAND

USSR

FINNMARK

Karasjok

Alta

SAUTSO

FINNMARKSVIDDA

LOPPA

FINLAND

Skjervøy

Kautokeino

RINGVASSØY

Lyngen

TROMSØ

KVALØYA

NORWEGIAN SEA

SENJA

TROMS

Bardu

Andenes

ANDØYA

Harstad

HINNØYA

Narvik

VESTERÅLEN

LANGØYA

Stokmarknes

SWEDEN

Svolvær
Brettesnes
Kabelvåg
Henningsvær
Stamsund

VESTVÅGØY

LOFOTEN ISLANDS

Reine

WEST FJORD

BLÅMANNSISEN
GLACIER

BODØ

SALTFJORD

NORWAY

Northern Half

0   15   30

Miles

SALT-FJELL

NORDLAND

SVARTISEN
GLACIER

ARCTIC CIRCLE

Mo

┼┼┼┼	Railway
——	Main Road
– – –	International Boundary

Mosjøen

VEGA

7

to Norway's.) The Caledonian folding and uplifting were accompanied by great volcanic activity, and volcanic intrusions – of quondam ash and lava – explain the region's wealth in granites and gneisses. In the Oslo region, fissures occurred in the earth's surface: large areas sank, up to 6000 feet, and the first fjords were formed. Geologically, all Norway is divided into three parts: the bedrock, the mountains and the Oslo region. In the last Ice Age, the land sank beneath the weight of ice: when it melted, some 10,000 years ago, the land again slowly rose. Today there are traces of ancient high-water marks as much as 2300 feet above sea-level.

Norway continues to rise, the rate in the Oslo Fjord being roughly a half-inch per annum. In the outer Oslo Fjord, close to Skjærhallen on the Hvaler islands, archaeologists have found the remains of a small village with a fishing-port. The settlement is believed to have been built around AD 1000: the harbour now lies 26 feet above sea-level.

Norway's largest lake, the Mjøsa, is an ancient fjord, very deep and far from the sea. In its depths the water is still salty and contains species normally found only in the ocean, krill as big as prawns, for example.

Glaciers are simply rivers of ice, but complicated by geographers with 'snouts', 'tongues' and 'end moraine'. In scientific research on the phenomenon (a branch of science pioneered by the Norwegian professor, Werner Werenskiold) the German term *Gletscher* appears to have been adopted internationally in preference to 'glacier'. The Norwegian for either is *isbre*. Glaciers are regarded as having 'firm areas' where the ice is compacted by the mass of covering snow, and 'melting areas' where, on 'outlet glaciers' or tongues, the summer sun melts both the snow-cover and the ice beneath. Not melting uniformly, the ice-masses crack – into the deep crevasses which, sometimes concealed beneath thin snow, are the dread of skiers and mountaineers. Competent guides are a vital requirement in such snow-covered mountain terrain.

Norway's largest glaciers are Jostedalsbreen in the province of Sogn and Fjordane (313 square miles); Svartisen (177 square miles) and, also in Nordland, Blåmannsisen (39 square miles); Hardangerjøkulen (37 square miles) and Folgefonna (85 square miles), both in Hordaland. Side by side, these would all still be dwarfed by Iceland's 3243-square-mile Vatnajøkul.

The moraine forced down by the weight of descending ice gouges out a depression which, if the ice later thaws, fills with melt-water. There results a glacier lake such as here below Nigardsbreen.

Nigardsbreen Glacier

Forests and Forestry. Wherever the mountain terrain permits, forests flourish. Twenty-seven per cent of Norway is covered by trees: spruce, pine and aspen, mountain ash, willow and birch. Working wood has since time immemorial been both an industry and an art: solid homes with elaborate façades, sturdy Viking ships finely carved fore and aft, magnificent stave churches. Even today some 100,000 farmers have forest as part of their property and operate it as an integral part of the farm. Large tracts are also owned by the state, along with private timber companies and the major landowners. Considerable investment in heavy machinery, the building of lumber roads and careful reafforestation ensure good returns both now and in the future.

Most of the produce of the forests goes to the manufacture of woodpulp, cellulose and paper, these being important exports. Norway is famous for its newsprint: most English-speaking readers of newspapers touch this Norwegian product every day. Company mergers and acquisitions have put much of this export business in the hands of a few large companies such as Norske Skog, Follum, Union and Orkla-Borregaard.

The spruce (of which the botanical name is *Picus norvegicus*) is Norway's leading species, followed by the pine. In recent years, however, wood from other than these evergreens has come to the fore as raw material for masonite and chipboard. Birchwood is now also popular, not only in homes, as logs for the fireplace, but also in industry as board for furniture and panelling.

Of Norway's total of 460 million cubic metres of timber – growing on approximately sixteen million acres – it is theoretically possible to cut about eleven million cubic metres per year. So far this limit has not been reached, but production is increasing steadily and will soon reach thirteen million cubic metres per annum. This increase results from improved treatment of the wood, and from research into and the use of new types of trees that grow faster. Large areas of forest are now fertilized, too.

There are some negative factors. Spruce-bug has on several occasions attacked, and acid rain from industrial neighbours to the east, south and west has affected the forests. Norway's own industry is also to blame, and the growing number of vehicles will, as in Germany, take their toll.

Paper derives very obviously from papyrus, on scrolls of which the Ancients kept their records until Bergama (antique Pergamon) gave its name to parchment (calf's hide) which, lying flat, could be bound into books. Rag 'paper' replaced hides as mediaeval writing matter until in 1844 the German textile-worker, Gottlob Keller, succeeded in dissolving fibre into wood-pulp.

After the Reformation, writing was no longer limited to that monopoly of the monasteries, copying manuscripts. Education was made more universal; printing presses appeared (and were often opposed); lay literature blossomed in 16th- and 17th-century Europe; newspapers evolved in the 18th century and from all this grew a major modern industry for which Norway became the world's foremost supplier. From Norwegian spruce come the newsprint, mechanical and chemical cellulose utilized in every corner of the globe.

Saugbrugsforeningen paper-works at Halden (above)
Stabbur – 'stave hut' – in the Telemark (above right)
Viking oak carving on the Oseberg Ship, Bygdøy (left)

10

Mammals and Reptiles. In Norway's forests lives Europe's largest land mammal, the elk or European moose. What Norwegians call the 'majestic king of the forest', or *elg*, is found throughout the country, but Hedmark and Oppland around Lake Mjøsa have by far the largest herds. In severe winters moose will wander into towns and cities, even Oslo. A fully grown bull can weigh up to half a ton – still only about half the weight of its North American cousin, the Giant moose.

Strangely enough, there are now more moose in Norway than ever before. This proliferation is a threat to the forests (fresh afforestation being trampled and/or eaten) and some 30,000 hunting permits are issued for moose each autumn (many to city-dwellers and foreigners at exorbitant prices). During the hunting season, ten-twelve times more moose are shot than 100 years ago. Moose and motor cars are a mutual traffic hazard: casualties for 1988 were 742 moose killed on the roads and 458 by train.

Since the War there has also been an increase in the numbers of that charming little deer, the roebuck (*rådyr*). Before 1940 these beautiful creatures were extremely rare but are now frequently seen, especially in winter. The roebuck has spread over most of the country – and with it, the lynx (whose favourite prey it is). Roebuck are equally vulnerable to vehicles: over 1000 are killed by cars each year.

The wolf (*ulv*) is often described as a voracious killer, even of human beings, and historically plays the rôle of the fearsome predator. Zoologists may have ascertained that the wolf does not merit such a reputation, but fixed ideas (and the farmers) still prevail. Norway has very few wolves (most being lone wolves straying in from Sweden) but every so often one is shot. It can safely be said that anyone coming here just to see wolves can almost certainly count on being disappointed.

There are on the other hand quite a few foxes – especially in Norwegian fairy-tales. The fox (*rev*) is no longer exclusively a forest-dweller but can also be seen in city suburbs. Near my office in Oslo, a few years ago, a female lived with six cubs only 50 yards from my window. Foxes will eat garbage and the contents of city dustbins, but prefer hares, small mammals like rats and mice, and especially fledge-lings such as young grouse. The diminutive but beautiful Mountain fox (*fjellrev*) is an endangered species and far from plentiful.

In western Norway and on the Trøndelag islands of Hitra and Frøya the handsome Red deer (*hjort*) is present in large numbers. The province of Møre and Romsdal has even more, and large-scale hunting is in consequence permitted.

The elk, *elg* or European moose, female and young

12

Attempts were made before the War to settle Musk oxen (*moskusdyr*) from Greenland in the Dovre area of central Norway. For a while it seemed the attempts would be successful, but not only the occupying Germans hunted the beefy animals so energetically that the project had to be repeated after the War. Now the herd in the Dovrefjell and Rondane mountains is such that lone bulls often come into conflict with the locals and have to be shot. At Bardu in Troms, a musk farm was started with a view to exporting the fine and costly inner wool that enables these animals to survive the arctic winter. Profits were however so low that the project collapsed.

The beautiful lynx or Norwegian leopard (*gaupe*) – with tufted ears – is the only wild member of the cat family living in Norway's forests (save for strayed domestic cats surviving in the wild). Lynx are especially fond of hares, but nowadays concentrate more and more on the proliferating roebuck. Sheep are even easier prey: with the large flocks unguarded, the lynx rarely lacks mutton, and arouses the wrath of sheep-owning farmers who want its numbers reduced.

The great Brown bear (*bjørn*) has returned to the forests (whence it also sallies forth to kill sheep on occasions). Its actual numbers are therefore contested, ecologists reckoning the Brown bears too few, farmers considering them too numerous, and proceeding to hunt them.

Reindeer, when one thinks of Norway, spring quite rightly to mind. The Lapps in northernmost Finnmark herd around 200,000 head of this tame but statuesque beast, the farmers in the eastern valleys rather less. Reindeer meat is increasing in popularity, even if polluted for quite some time after Chernobyl. Mobile butchering units have been introduced to ensure that reindeer-meat reaches the markets in prime condition.

Wild reindeer (*villrein*) survive from prehistoric times and in abundance (again by the negative evidence of the number of hunting permits issued: 25,000 annually). These were the beasts that our ancestors hunted, setting traps on the Hardanger and other high plateaux in southern Norway and the Trøndelag. As you walk along the marked paths of the Hardangervidda, several hundred reindeer may come down the mountainside and some stand, unforgettably, a yard or two away.

Like the fox, the black and white badger (*grevling*) has moved to town. Large and heavy, it moves mainly by night, like a tank across the road. Villa-owners do not generally enthuse over badgers that upturn dustbins noisily at night. Badgers often hibernate under piles of leaves, or in outhouses on the outskirts of the city.

Smaller members of the marten family resident here are the marten itself, of which about 10,000 are shot or trapped each year, and wild mink, some 26,000 of which are bagged annually. The latter descend from fugitives from badly fenced mink farms, and are playing havoc with the fish in Norway's lakes.

That lithe and likeable creature, the otter (*oter*), is another member of the marten family. It is found over most of the country, especially close inshore and in rivers. It eats fish, frogs and smaller rodents but also takes the blame for killing the occasional lamb. Otter-skin is beautiful and deservedly expensive. Popes in the Middle Ages apparently permitted otter-meat to be eaten on Friday and during Lent – as 'fish' because of its slightly fishy smell. The species is now completely protected throughout Norway.

The ermine (*røyskatt*) and its little brother, the Snow mouse, are much sought after for their winter fur. Ermine is supposedly 'an emblem of honour and purity' – and also used in the robes of judges and peers.

A recent immigrant is the Marten dog (*mårhund*), which has found its way to Norway from Russia. Sighted only very rarely, it belongs to the dog family and is sometimes called 'Chinese racoon'.

Some of Norway's oldest place-names begin with *bjor-*, *bjør-* or *bjur-*, indicating that this, the beaver, is a well-known resident of long standing. It is also Norway's largest rodent and an energetic builder in many southern rivers.

It would be wrong to say that the beaver is as popular with farmers and fishermen as it is with tourists and nature-lovers. Its pelt was in great demand, so much so that the beaver was on the point of extinction in Scandinavia when, in 1899, it became a protected species. Reintroduced into its old breeding grounds, the beaver as a species has

The wolverine (*jerv*), the largest member of the marten family, is hated and feared wherever it is found – in the USA, Canada and Alaska also. The wolverine walks flat-footed like a bear, but even in mountain terrain can outrun and kill its favourite prey, the reindeer. Wolverines are reputed to kill not simply for food, but far in excess of this viz. for the sake of killing.

Lemmings sometimes breed in such numbers that, like the Vikings before them, they burst their boundaries. In teeming columns they march seaward, drowning en masse in rivers and finally – not suicidally but by sheer weight of numbers – in the ocean. The lemming army feeds a camp-following of predatory birds and animals. Such carnivores proliferate in the years of the lemmings' migrations; smaller species of birds and mammals thrive too because, feeding amply on the lemming, hawks and large predators leave them to breed in peace.

In the last twenty years considerable research has been carried out in Norway on lemmings and the various short-tailed mice. One finding is that the lemmings' mass migration seems to coincide with a rise in the numbers of mice. When the latter become too numerous and overcrowd their territory, the lemmings' adrenalin appears to increase, provoking their 'suicidal' rush.

Snowy owl

bounced back. There are now so many in Norway that they have to be culled – and the tasty meat served in better restaurants during the hunting season. Very few hunting permits are however issued for beaver.

Endearing as its Norwegian name may be – *pinnsvin* (pin-pig) – the hedgehog is all too often flattened by traffic, and this wandering pincushion is now seen (alive) less and less. The species is protected, and the subject of research projects financed by the World Wide Fund for Nature.

Norway is also home to many types of rats and mice. The species that brought the Black Death to Bergen in 1349 was the Black rat, followed in the 1700s by the *Rattus norvegicus*. Nowadays, its best-known relative is the lemming (*lemen*), a rodent so small as to be scarcely noticeable to the human eye.

The long-legged hare (*hare*, too, in Norwegian) is a beautiful creature that is for all that a popular target during the long hunting season. In winter it is white, in summer brown. Skiing through the forest, one frequently sees its tracks – sometimes even the signs of nocturnal encounters between this fast-footed rodent and the ever-present fox.

The squirrel (*ekorn*) has inhabited Norway's forests for as long as man. One king, Harald Gråfell (Greypelt), even took his name from its fur. Squirrel-pelts were formerly exported in bulk throughout Europe, and the meat left to be eaten by hungry Norwegians. Squirrels are the favourite prey of many predators, and are themselves as partial to birds' eggs and chicks as they are to hazel-nuts.

Norway has only one species of venomous snake, and not a very venomous one at that. It is the viper, which feeds on lemmings and other small rodents and sometimes little birds. Most people are more frightened of the viper than they should be. It no doubt plays its part in the natural cycle. The other two species of snake here are not poison-ous, but are frequently killed 'just in case'.

The skink is completely harmless and really not a snake at all but a lizard without legs. Two types of newt occur in certain natural and man-made lakes; lizards are found in southern Norway especially, and there are two kinds of frog and one of toad.

Birds. Norway is blessed with many birds of many species. At the risk of shocking ornithologists (and not ashamed of my overriding interest in food), I shall put the tastiest first: the ptarmigan (*rype*), delicious when served with *tyttebær* (lingon or cranberries), and its relatives the woodcock, partridge, grouse and capercailye. Some sea-birds are eaten as well: ducks, geese, cormorants and the razor-billed auk. Other species like snipe and ruff also end up on Norwegian tables, as do quite a few larger thrushes and pigeons. Unlike the French, though, Nor-wegians never eat smaller songbirds.

Off the coasts of western and northern Norway stand a number of bird-rocks where sea-birds nest in thousands. Such colonies consist principally of gull and tern species, cormorants and guillemots. While the puffin population is dropping – due to the decrease in herring and capelin – eiders are increasing along the whole coast south to the Swedish border. The underplumage of the eider – its down – is of course the source of what Britons slept under until they discovered duvets.

Eastern Norway boasts not only Grey Lag and Dwarf geese. The Canada geese seen in a high, snow-plough-shaped fly-past are

Dotterel

Ptarmigan, cock in early spring plumage

Eider eggs in a nest of down

Fulmar nesting on Runde Island

descendants of the pairs brought to the Nesodden peninsula outside Oslo by an enterprising farmer before the War. They land in hundreds on the bays around Oslo and spend the winter there.

It has been a pleasure to note the advances swans have made. At Eidsvoll, not far north of Oslo, the River Vorma is full of them in the boating season. They are plentiful, too, on that birdwatcher's paradise, Lake Øyeren; on the wetlands of Østfold, in the lower stretches of the River Glomma and on the Hvaler islands. It is not unusual to see swans with eight-ten cygnets paddling majestically on the small bays and mini-fjords of that island delight.

The smaller but equally beautiful Whooper swans also fly in formation over southern Norway, en route for Siberia and other points north. Their Norwegian name is *sangsvane* (singing swan) which may, like Greenland, have been a discoverer's joke, for their call is less song-like than nose-blowing honk.

On certain wetlands the crane is now returning annually from its migrations south. It stands, very stately, four feet tall. On quiet lakes and ponds the striking grebe/loon makes its nest on a floating island of plants, alongside various types of duck – and a growing number of gulls. The last were before the War almost exclusively sea-birds but are now present over most of the mountain area inland. They are carriers of a harmful parasite which is spreading to trout and other freshwater fish.

Norway is one of the few remaining countries in which the eagle is not only no longer endangered but safely re-established. Both the Golden eagle and the even larger White-tailed eagle are now nesting here and breeding – to the satisfaction of ornithologists but the chagrin of the local population. The latter, at Leka in North Trøndelag, recall an incident in 1932 when an eagle carried off a four-year-old girl to its eyrie 1000 feet up. Its victim, a certain Svanhild, lived (and still lives) to tell the tale. Ornithologists are however sceptical, on the grounds that a child's weight exceeds an eagle's carrying capacity. The controversy caused so much public interest that in 1979 a committee was set up in Leka to vindicate Svanhild.

The largest of Norway's many hawks is the osprey, nicknamed 'fish-eagle' though not of the eagle family. Several types of falcon inhabit the mountains – and in the Middle Ages all belonged to the king. Falconry was the sport of kings; Håkon Håkonsson had many falconers to train these birds, which served also as much appreciated gifts from one crowned head to another.

Nowadays falcons are in very short supply. People drive in surreptitiously with specially built cars to steal the eggs for hatching and sale overseas. Arab shaikhs pay high prices for well-trained falcons, and efforts are being made to protect birds from these human predators.

Owls abound. The largest is the Eagle or Great Horned owl, so called because of its ear-tufts or 'horns'. The species was near extinction but, saved with the help of the World Wide Fund for Nature, it is now multiplying again. Worth mentioning also is the pretty Snowy owl, which turns shiny white in winter.

Efforts to protect endangered species are often hindered in this country by those who believe that domestic animals and even children are themselves endangered by wildlife. Understanding for this vital environmental issue is however growing, with politicians increasingly mindful of future generations. Most of us feel that enabling our children and grandchildren to discover and appreciate nature, to have regard for

Known in Norwegian as *lundefugl*, 'lunde-fowl', puffins gave Devon's Lundy Island its name

Kittiwakes nesting, Runde Island

the creatures that share this planet with them, is more important than many other so-called principles. In Norway there is a special *Miljøvern-departement* (Ministry of the Environment) responsible for conservation and working closely with both international organizations like the World Wide Fund for Nature and Norwegian universities, research institutes and the *Naturvernforbund* (Nature Conservation Association).

On Spitsbergen, the group of arctic islands administered by Norway, millions of sea-birds congregate each summer; but few, save the ptarmigans, stay to share the rigours of winter with the endemic polar bears, foxes, seals, walruses and the islands' species of squat and rotund reindeer.

Sea-, Shell- and Freshwater fish. Crustacea probably provided our earliest forebears with the wherewithal to survive: mussels, cockles and the other molluscs they found along the beach. There is ample archaeological evidence of this. Norway's long coast-line is rich in such delicacies,

Low-tide rock-pools, Lofoten coast

which modern restaurants appreciate quite as much as ancient man. They are none the less more usual on Mediterranean tables than in Norway where far more are grown. Here quality is high in mussels, oysters and scallops (the last in four different varieties), to mention only a few. Norwegians may produce excellent cockles and export them profitably to the rest of Europe, but themselves disdain them as fit only for bait.

Conches, whelks (which Norwegians call 'trumpet-snails', *trompet-snegl*) and limpets (*albueskjell* – 'elbow shells') are also pooh-poohed. Our ancestors found them not only delicious, but also essential eating. But then they ate seaweed too, like the Japanese.

Shrimp here are worth writing home about, both smaller scampi (for potted shrimps etc.) and the larger prawns caught by trawlers. Given its Latin name *Nephrops norvegicus*, Norwegians have taken a remarkably long time to discover how delectable crayfish are. Before the War there was scarcely a market for these strange spiny lobsters, but now their price is rising faster than that of shrimp.

Lobsters in Norway might be thought to be blushing at the price nowadays asked for them, far higher than in Britain or the USA. (They are in fact red only when cooked.) The answer might be to farm them commercially, if only lobsters were not so partial to lobster-meat too.

A new product of the ocean on its way to our pots is a tiny member of the shrimp family called krill. It exists in astonishing quantities along Norway's coasts, especially in the polar region. Here it was the main food of the great schools of whales, until they were decimated.

Another source of sea-food has until recently been used only as bait (mainly for hooking a small shark – *pigghå* – which is exported as *chien de mer*). I mean the *akkar* or squid, calamar. This marine ingredient features in recipes of every country and culture. Norwegians, however, are so averse to eating it that squid is the only fish that, as mere 'bait', is subject to VAT. Around the Mediterranean, another favourite of both ancient and modern man is the sea-urchin. Norway has plenty, but I have never heard of their being eaten here.

It is said that the uglier a fish looks the better it tastes – a rule proved by the exception of such beautiful and delectable varieties as the salmon, trout and mackerel. Species on the other hand confirming the rule are the gruesome monk-fish and ocean cat-fish, not forgetting the turbot and perhaps the halibut too.

Norway's most respected, even revered species are the Atlantic salmon and its smaller cousin, the sea-trout. Both come to Norwegian rivers to spawn. So many, however, were until recently caught en route, with so few survivors arriving, that the government prohibited salmon- and trout-fishing at sea and in the estuaries. This had an immediate effect and by 1989 the spawning grounds were fully active and the rivers well stocked. Fish-farming then created an unexpected problem: 'tame' salmon escaping from fish-farm nets fertilized wild species and caused some genetic confusion. More serious – and still unresolved – is the hazard of special salmon diseases which the one often passes to the other.

During the last 200 years British and Irish anglers have converged every summer on the best salmon rivers in western and northern Norway. Some became legends, like the Duke of Westminster and the Alta River, or a certain Mr White who in the 1860s paid 2000 dollars for hunting and fishing rights to the north-western island of Loppa (the Flea) but found he had bought the whole island by mistake.

Winter fishing off the Lofotens

Throughout the ages Norway's most important sea-fish have without a doubt been cod and herring. These were essential for prehistoric man's survival in this harsh and often barren land. Herring were traditionally salted before being exported to other European countries. Cod-fish and the like were split and hung to dry – on racks in the Lofotens and northern Norway, on rocks in the west – then sent to mainly the Latin countries as raw material for several national dishes (in particular *bacalao*, this being Spanish for cod).

Norwegians are very fond of cod, particularly relishing the roe and liver which they sometimes boil with vinegar as a sauce for the fish. Here cod often becomes the celebrated *lutefisk,* lye-fish. The stockfish (or rack-dried cod) is soaked in an alkaline solution (lye). (For Norwegian communities in the States it is dried into solid hunks, which have to be sawn up – and the smelly sawdust swept away.) It is then boiled into a jelly-like mass and eaten principally for the traditional Christmas dinner, which Norwegians enjoy on the evening of 24 December. The continuing popularity of lye-fish amongst American Norwegians disproves the suspicion that the smell of it boiling was the reason for their originally emigrating.

Loading the Lofoten cod-racks

Salmon jumping

Black bearberry and Reindeer moss

Government campaigns against pollution have worked very well in some rivers. Waters in which nothing lived a few years ago now teem with salmon and trout. Even in Oslo, the Akerselv or River Aker now boasts fifteen species. Salmon ladders are being built on many watercourses to bring the fish to higher spawning grounds.

Besides trout and salmon, the 'king and crown prince', other members of the salmon family are found here in lakes and rivers. In Lake Mjøsa, Norway's largest, live trout weighing up to 30 pounds.

Smaller lakes are often rich in perch: loved by a few but detested by far more because of its many tiny bones. A large predator, the pike occurs in lakes and certain rivers: it is seldom eaten in Norway although considered a delicacy in Sweden. I remember my grandmother cooking it with its tail tucked between its crocodile-like teeth. Pike is the raw material for the famous *quenelles* of French cuisine.

The mackerel is a popular species, except in northern Norway (where a superstition survives that the brown meat along its backbone is human flesh). The mackerel is sometimes called the chicken of the sea, a gastronomic compliment challenged by the whiting which, when boiled and served with parsley butter, is delicious.

The capelin (caplin or capelan – *lodde*) is a small herring-like member of the salmon family that played until recently an important part in Norway's fishing economy. Annually from February to April it moves south to northern Finnmark to spawn. There, in vast shoals (the townsfolk of Vadsø would scoop them out by net), the capelin attracted the cod which in turn attracted most of northern Norway's fishing-fleet.

Plenty of flounder is fished off Norway, as well as several varieties of sole, plaice, turbot and their bigger relative, the halibut (which costs even more than salmon). Also caught is skate/ray, the 'wings' of which are thought highly of on the Continent and are at last catching on in Oslo's restaurants.

Other fish which in Norwegian were earlier dismissed as *ufisk* ('unfish') are now mixed with crab-meat and turbot as popular 'crabfish' products. In fierce competition with the Japanese, these excellent seafoods are now processed in Norway and exported.

Mention has been made of fish-farms. In a very short space of time these have developed from the hobby of a few – mostly landlubbers – to a major export industry. Fish-farms now produce some 100,000 tons annually for export, mainly of salmon but also of trout. Most is exported frozen or chilled, some smoked or cured.

Many other types of fish are now appearing on the market. Eel from the fish-farms enjoys increasing popularity, and 'farmed' turbot and halibut will, one hopes, sell for less.

The subject of fishing should not be concluded without a word of tribute: not only to the generations of Norwegians who have spent long icy months at sea, often facing arctic storms in tiny boats, but to modern technicians whose ingenuity has opened up new markets and brought new wealth. Throughout the world consumers who might not buy just 'fish' are attracted to 'ocean-fresh' fillets, fish-fingers, fish-sticks and fish-balls (which, to avoid deliberate misconstruction, are sold in America as 'fishmeat-balls'). The small shark caught with the help of the squid is beautifully packaged and sold to France as *chien de mer* (dog of the sea) – by Norwegians who would never dream of eating it themselves. Some is also exported to Denmark (where it is cleverly smoked and resold as 'ocean eel').

Purple saxifrage

Dwarf cornel

Agriculture. That Norway is a beautiful country is, if anything, compensation for the lack of ease and convenience of life there. Other than in Lista and Jæren, around the Oslo Fjord, the Trondheim Fjord and Lake Mjøsa, the mountains are in command. Often the great massifs are cut by deep V-shaped fjords, making communication difficult and costly, and increasing the north's dependence, in particular, on the coastal steamer, the *Hurtigruta*.

Agricultural land is consequently limited; only three per cent of Norway is arable. The admixture of silt washed down from the mountains makes however for fertility and results in fine crops in good years. It is often claimed that fruit and berries have a finer aroma and general quality when ripened further north. Evidence the strawberries from the Trondheim area and cloudberries from the heart of Troms, above the Arctic Circle. Cranberries, bear-, blue-, bill-, cloud-, cow- and crowberries . . . Norway boasts many little known elsewhere.

In earlier days, agriculture was directly dependent on domestic animals. It was their manure which, spread on the fields in late winter then ploughed in, fertilized the soil. The introduction of artificial fertilizers revolutionized life on the farm, enabling grain to be grown extensively, and in certain regions exclusively.

Norway's cattle have developed, thanks to research and enriched cattle-feeds, from the Dagros of old into the popular modern strain known as NRF (Norwegian Red cattle). The average NRF cow produces

Vesterålen farming

Horses, now used less and less on the farm, have during the last few years again found their place in the forests. In rugged and wooded mountain terrain the horse beats the motor car, however many horse-powered.

Norway has three traditional types: the *fjording* (the West Norwegian or Fjord-horse), the *dølahest* (Valley horse) and the *lyngshest* or North Norwegian horse. Resident here since time immemorial, the Fjord-horse is distinctive in both appearance and colouring, being almost always 'dirty gold'. During the last 25 years so many Fjord-horse studs have been exported to the USA, Denmark, the Netherlands and elsewhere that they now outnumber those left in the mother country.

The Valley horse appeared in its present guise in the 1750s. After four years' duty on the borders of Holstein on behalf of the Danish-Norwegian king, Norwegian troops returned home with a few Holstein stallions. With the help of Valley-horse mares (which at that time looked probably not unlike the long-established Fjord-horse), they produced a larger breed, stronger for working but less amenable to the saddle.

The Lyngs- or North Norwegian horse, though ancient, would have become extinct but for the efforts of a few energetic and dedicated equestrians. Equally well suited for driving, the Lyngshorse is a popular mount, and its numbers are fast increasing. Foreign breeds such as the Iceland horse and New Forest pony, and larger mounts from Great Britain, Ireland, Germany and Poland are imported in considerable numbers. Interest in horses is soaring, especially amongst the young, with equestrian centres proliferating both in city suburbs and rural areas.

It is finally worth mentioning that a new race has been bred from the Iceland horse. Though small, it is never called a pony because it is a direct descendant of the horse the Vikings rode. It is quick and elegant, boasting a distinctive gait named *tølt* – a way of walking faster than most horses trot. Breeding is concentrated in the province of Møre and Romsdal, around Vestnes in the Romsdal Valley.

about 8800 pints per annum – some require a special 'bra' to keep their udders off the ground. Far fewer cows (now under 400,000) now yield far more milk for a shorter working day. Only 63,000 Norwegians or thereabouts are at present registered as raising cattle, sheep or goats. (Registration entails ownership of at least 2½ acres of arable land and an annual minimum of 36½ days' work on the land.) NRF bulls are much sought after world-wide for enhancing breeding stock for both milk and meat. Besides experimenting successfully with pure beef types like France's Charolais, scientists are bringing back the old Norwegian Telemark cow by an intricate system of breeding.

Sheep, usually unattended, graze Norway's mountains and hillsides to the tune of over 2·2 million. Losses during grazing amount to five per cent: while shepherds seem inseparable from their flocks elsewhere, few Norwegians tend theirs, and the loss of over 100,000 sheep annually is appalling. Attempts are always made to blame carnivorous wild animals and birds, but the few remaining eagles, bears, lynx, wolverines and wolves can scarcely account for so many sheep. There is however a new trend now towards herding flocks more efficiently. Norwegian shepherd's dogs are being cross-bred with good sheep-dogs from Scotland, and demand for their progeny is increasing.

Goats we know from Norse mythology. When the god of war, Thor, drove his goat-drawn chariot over the heavens, thunder was heard. When his two goats were butchered and eaten by the gods at night, their bare bones placed inside their empty hides resulted in a healthy resurrection the next morning. The successors of Thor's animals are still seen on mountainsides and in the most remote valleys, but far less than in earlier days: only 75,000 head of Norway's Emerald goat are reckoned to survive. Goat's milk is more nutritious than cow's but is little used save in Norway's famous *geitost*, the sweet and caramelly goat's cheese that features on every breakfast buffet.

Wood crane's bill

Livelong saxifrage

Halden's paper and wood-pulp plant

Pigs were part and parcel of the Norseman's household, even in pre-Christian times. They figure prominently in Nordic mythology, and today one can say without *arrière-pensée* that there are more pigs in Norway than ever before: over 700,000. Pigs have developed to such a degree that they lack most of the fat that our forefathers needed during long freezing winters. Breeding has been aimed at longish animals providing streaky bacon – more acceptable to a weight-watching and cholesterol-conscious public. In some countries pig-rearing has reached industrial proportions and, in order to protect themselves from 'big pig farmers', Norwegian pressure groups have successfully lobbied parliament for a law limiting the number of pigs to 500 per farm.

Poultry is subject to similar official restrictions. Norwegians are allowed to own only 2000 laying hens and to keep in their broiler-houses no more than 25,000 fowl. (In neighbouring countries one commonly sees broiler-farms of several hundred thousand hens, and some with an annual total of more than one million.) Which is why the price of a broiler-chicken in Norway is twice that of Sweden and three times that in Denmark. The last ten years have seen more hens in Norway than ever before, but fewer roosters. There are now as many laying hens as broilers, about 5½ million of each; although consumption of the latter has shot up, it still lags behind that of comparable countries.

Turkeys are relatively few – about 75,000 – but the figure is rising as Norwegians switch from the traditional pig (or lye-fish) to turkey on Christmas Eve, the great time for family feasting. In addition, about 4000 ducks and 5000 geese are eaten annually.

Mining, Industry, Shipping and Oil. Waterfalls – which Norway does not lack – have since the Middle Ages been used to drive sawmills and mill-wheels. These became literally the country's motive force. Factories soon lined the rivers like pearls on a string, luring labourers away from the land. Mining, especially for iron, dates from prehistoric times. Improved in the last century by mechanisation and the use of explosives, the mines have recently fallen on hard times, due to smaller lodes and cheaper sources overseas. This has led to economic problems in communities centred on a single mine or commodity. At Kirkenes, activity is almost at a standstill on the miles of mountainside grey and scarred from open-cast iron-mining. The coal is still coming out of Spitzbergen, however, and at Eidsvoll the old gold-works, closed for 90 years, has become a tourist attraction. Here visitors are welcomed to dig for gold, and try their hand at panning nuggets from the sand.

The first trade unions appeared at the turn of the century and soon made their presence felt. By the 1920s the Labour movement had become very strong; the first Labour government was returned in 1927 but lasted only three weeks. The crash of 1929 and the ensuing Depression affected Norway equally: unemployment rose and living conditions deteriorated. Strikes and lock-outs became common, and many feared a Communist revolution. In 1935, Johan Nygaardsvold took over with a strong minority government and the slogan 'The whole nation at work'.

The waterfalls that first powered Norway's dark Satanic mills had over the years been harnessed to provide cheap electricity. This encouraged the development along the fjords of heavy industry: cheaply-powered and competitive exports such as chemicals and fertilizers helped Norway back on to its feet. By the time the War struck so suddenly, it looked as though the Nygaardsvold slogan had come true.

Before and for some time after the War, industry had been divided into what were known as the 'home' and 'export' sectors. Norway's 'home industries' had been protected by tariffs: though in line with OECD and GATT levels, duty on imported goods was high. In the 1950s these trade barriers came down. Many factories meeting demand at home only were now forced to seek new markets overseas. In a very short space of time the 'home sector' was outselling, overseas, the old 'export' producers of such unlikely lines as radios and recorders.

Workers now left the land and found jobs in the factories, with industry replacing agriculture as the country's main revenue-earner. Manufactured products new amongst Norway's exports were furniture ('Scandinavian design'), pleasure-craft, data equipment, paints, plastics and deep-frozen foods. Traditional exports prospered also: newsprint and other paper products, chemicals and aluminium. The mighty conglomerate Norsk Hydro (the Norwegian Hydro-electric Company) diversified and took on international stature.

The key factor in Norway's recent economic history has, of course, been oil. In the early 1950s Norway's own Council for Geological Research told a Geneva conference on ocean rights that 'One can disregard the possibilities of finding oil, gas or sulphur in the continental shelf along the Norwegian coast'. When Phillips Petroleum approached Trygve Lie on the subject in 1962, he replied 'I believe you must have made a mistake. Norway has no oil or gas'. By 1964 – when it was ruled that the North Sea's deep Norwegian Trench was an 'accidental geological crevice' (to which Norway could therefore claim sea-bed mineral rights) – seventeen companies had been licensed to search for off-shore oil. The Ekofisk field was found in 1969 and came on stream in 1971. Now the production of the seven Ekofisk oil- and gas-fields is more than double Norway's needs. One of Europe's poorest nations had suddenly found itself rich.

The Norwegian merchant navy had been reduced to half its strength by the Germans, and after the War an intensive rebuilding programme began. Norway rapidly rose amongst the world's shipping nations from number five to number three. A crisis came with the 1980s: rising costs destroyed competitiveness and the fleet was cut, shipowners either going bankrupt or having to 'flag out', under flags of convenience, in order to survive.

Then the famous NIS – the new Norwegian Shipping Register – was drawn up and over 700 owners had soon 'flagged in' again. The tanker fleet increased capacity; cargo too became profitable. The merchant navy began recruiting officers again, lower ranks being filled mainly by foreigners willing to work for lower wages. In 1990 Norway was back to its former world-position of shipowning nation number five. An expanding cruise-ship fleet is proving very successful: here owners like the Knut Kloster father and son, the Wilhelmsen brothers, the Skaugen brothers and – the best known internationally – Fred Olsen and his daughter Annette have been the pioneers.

Another major industry is aviation. Norway owns two sevenths of SAS (the Scandinavian Airline System) and is proud of the achievements of its own family-firm, Braathen S.A.F.E. High-street travel agencies, charter flights and package holidays are the modern endorsement of an old Norse song: *Norrøna folket, det vil fare*', 'The Norwegian people will travel'.

Norway's past

Prehistoric. Where the first Norwegians came from we do not really know, but anthropologists agree that a race of hunters existed here over 20,000 years ago, well before the last Ice Age. Fragments of mammoth skeletons, found also in Siberia and Alaska, indicate how our forebears lived and what they ate. Before organizing themselves to hunt such big game, they eked out an existence on mussels, cockles and other low-tide pickings.

After the Ice Ages, Norway is thought to have been further peopled by immigrants from three main directions: most came from the south through the present-day province of Østfold; others over the North Sea to western Norway – to establish what is known as the Fosna Culture – and a third group from the east, to found the so-called Komsa Culture which spread south and left traces on the Hardanger Plateau. The carbon-14 method of testing has made it possible to date these first settlers to 7000-5000 BC.

In the south (but also as far north as the Lofoten Islands) they left behind numbers of Neolithic (i.e. later Stone Age) artefacts, from 4000-1500 BC. Tools were made from rocks and wood. With time, the axes became sharper; clay pots were introduced for cooking.

By 1500 BC Norway was ready for the Bronze Age (unlike early man in America, who moved from the Neolithic to the Iron Age). Bronze (an alloy of copper and tin) did not make for axes any sharper than could be chipped from flints, so forests were still burned, rather than cut, and crops planted in the ashes. The keeping of livestock increased. While good finds from the Stone Age are scarce, archaeologists have discovered well-endowed Bronze-age graves equipped with a rich and interesting array of domestic items, weapons and gold and silver artefacts.

When iron-smelting reached Norway's shores – about 500 BC – forests could be cut down and agriculture improved. Iron-age burial rites were however different, and graves from this period yield much less and inferior material. Now man here lived from animal husbandry, agriculture, hunting and fishing – as he would for centuries to come.

Rock engravings – presumed evidence of prehistoric man in Norway – have been found in 40-odd locations, some associated with ancient cults and rites. The most significant are at Alta in the Finnmark province and – nearer home, close to the main E6 highway – at Skjeberg in Østfold. The extensive areas worked on flat, smooth rock, usually covered (and protected?) by moss or turf, are classified as *veideristing* (hunting scenes) or *jordbruksristing* (agricultural scenes). The latter include depictions of persons, animals, wagons and ships, footprints, sun-wheels and sexual organs, and activities such as battles, horse-racing, wedding parties and ploughing. The *veideristing* were probably designed to invoke super-natural help towards a successful hunt. Though free of perspective and any sense of composition, such prehistoric rock art provides a forthright statement, clear and untendentious, on the way of life and (pre)occupations of our early ancestors. (The russet color-ation is not prehistoric painting but a modern visual aid.)

Remotely Roman. There is in Norway plentiful evidence of trade and contact with the Roman world. Weapons as well as glass and bronze articles found their way to these remote regions so far from Rome. The still-visible foundations of buildings from this period indicate that in most cases an extended family would inhabit one large farm. The practice seems to have been also to bury one or two persons (possibly elders) from each generation in a grave decorated with circular stones, and to enclose each property with a stone wall.

It is known that many a local chieftain must have been extremely rich. At Haram in the Sunnmøre district of Møre and Romsdal as much as 620 grams of gold were found in a single grave. Similar sites also gave up scythes, axes, adzes and other implements little changed from then till now. Our harnesses, stirrups, bits and spurs are rarely as richly adorned as those found in Norway's Iron-age graves. The later Iron Age in particular (which in Norway preceded and succeeded the Roman period – from 500 BC to AD 800) produced a very high standard of ornamentation and craftsmanship in silver and gold. By then Germanic influences were evident in the form of well-designed animal- and plant-motifs.

It was always thought that our earliest ancestors took several millennia to move from isolated family-farms into communities. Norway's first towns were, according to the history-books, founded about 1000 years ago. In the light of recent remarkable finds near Stavanger, the history-books may have to be rewritten. Excavations on farmland at Forsandmoen in Ryfylke have in the last ten years revealed a sizeable village of some 70 'town houses' 3500 years old. When Troy fell, Norwegians were already living in orderly communities, their large heated long-houses adjoined by outbuildings and efficient pens for several hundred cattle. A similar settlement has also just been excavated at Borg in the Lofoten Islands, one house measuring 7000 square feet.

The Vikings vindicated. Until very recently it was customary to dismiss, or at most deprecate our Viking ancestors. Contemporary congregations prayed to be spared the *furor Normanorum*. 'Crude, brutal and barbarous' are terms still commonly heard. We now however have archaeological and other evidence that gives a very different picture of these Nordic warriors and their way of life. The BBC's well-known Viking expert, Magnus Magnusson, himself of Icelandic origin, said of the excavation of the Viking town of Jorvik (York) that the notorious Eric Bloodaxe was 'the most slandered king in history'. At Jorvik there was not a single weapon among the 17,000 items found. The same was true in Dublin (a Viking town founded by Olav the White). Both became notable centres of craftsmanship and trade, as is amply demonstrated by the museum site at York and the collections in Dublin's historical museum.

Every spring from around the year 800 until the mid-11th century, Norsemen from Viken (the Oslo Fjord) and other coastal areas as far north as Hålogaland would 'go viking', as they say. A local chief or 'sea-king' would lead an expedition consisting of a single ship or small flotilla. All on board were free and equal (except the cook, a serf), and booty was divided evenly, once the shipowner had received his share.

Easy prey for these freebooters were the churches, monasteries and small towns further south. (Monasteries were the banks of the time,

Prow of the Oseberg Ship, in the Viking Ship Museum, Bygdøy, Oslo

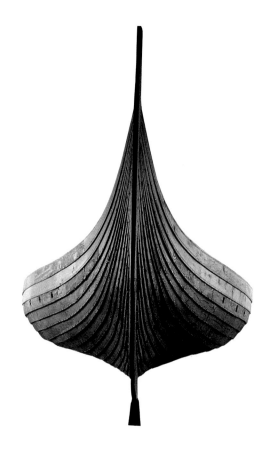

which well-to-do citizens entrusted with their valuables.) Slaves as well as valuables were Viking objectives, and thousands of young English, Irish and Scottish men and women were brought back to Norway. The inevitable effect on each new generation's genes needs no elaboration.

As time went by, the Vikings came to stay for longer periods in the places they had first raided. Settling, they turned from warring to less demanding activities such as commerce and handicrafts, as the finds at Jorvik and Dublin show.

The Vikings' first appearance in written history is not civilized but violent. On 8 June 793 they raided the monastery of Lindisfarne or Holy Island. Another rich and influential monastery, at Armagh, was seized by a Norse leader called Torgils who, installing his wife as soothsayer, proceeded to seize large parts of Ireland. He ruled for seventeen years, until his Irish subjects drowned him in the Shannon. Subsequent Viking incursions into Ireland were twofold. Not only did the first waves of raiders arrive from Norway without their womenfolk, to settle and intermarry; the Norsemen who descended, geographically and over several generations, to the Normans of north-west France continued their migratory curve into Ireland. Evidence the Fitz- – the old French *fils de*, 'son of' – that precedes the Geralds, Patricks and Simmons in older Irish names.

Ireland, northern England and Scotland were in the 9th and 10th centuries the scene of stabler, more advanced and better documented Norse civilization than Norway itself. In the homeland, Norwegians have their most detailed early history from the Icelandic sagas.

The Olav the White who founded Dublin is thought to have had a brother Ivar, whose descendants ruled Ireland until 1016. Whether both were sons of the southern Norwegian king, Gudred of Agder, or of Gudred Veidekonge (Geoffrey the Hunter) is disputed, and of interest to very few. More significant is the recent belief that Olav is the king found buried in the Gokstad ship that still astonishes visitors to Bygdøy. Olav's wife was one Aud the Deep-eyed, and their son Torstein the Red; he conquered large parts of Scotland, married a certain Turid and died in 875. The familiar Scottish Mac derives from the Norse prefix 'son of' viz. MacIvor (son of Ivar), Macaulay (son of Olav) and MacLaughlin, son of the man from the lakeland i.e. Norway.

We know from school that Anglo-Saxon England was invaded and in part ruled by the Danes. Under Svein Forkbeard and King Cnut (Canute), thousands of Norwegian Vikings served in the 'Great Army', as the Danish occupation force was called. Second-in-command under King Svein was Olav Tryggvason, who later returned to conquer Norway (and found Trondheim). On the other hand, his relative Olav Haraldsson (St Olav) fought with the English against the Danes, one engagement being commemorated in the ditty 'London Bridge is falling down' . . . which it did, with the Danish troops on it, when Olav tied his boats to its supports and ordered his crews to row off.

Only one town in Norway is known to predate the year 1000: Tunsberg (Tønsberg), which was supposedly built in 871. Borg (later Sarpsborg) was founded by St Olav in 1016. The most important Viking centre (and possibly the only one that might be called a town) was Jorvik: around 950, during the reign of Eric Bloodaxe, it had about 10,000 inhabitants. Oslo was built in 1050 by the last Viking king, Harald Hardråde.

Our knowledge of the Vikings having started in England, at Lindisfarne in 793, it is nice to note that it ended there too. On 25 September

Viking craftsmanship: silver fibula, gold bracelet, buttons and brooch, in Oslo University's Museum of National Antiquities

1066, Harald Hardråde was killed at the battle of Stamford Bridge. With his defeat, and the Norman Conquest three weeks later, the Vikings ceased to wield their dreaded double-axe over north-western Europe.

Of the thousands of Scandinavians who 'went viking' to the east, founding the princedom of Gardariket (near modern Novgorod and Kiev), most were Swedes. Many came from Roslagen, east of present-day Stockholm, and were known as *Ros*. The eastern princedom they established was in consequence called *Rossia*, and this – in Russian – is still the name of the largest Russian republic. The Norse kings Olav Tryggvason, Harald Hardråde, St Olav and Magnus the Good were all guests of their relatives at the court of Kiev. Harald Hardråde went even further, to Mikligardr, *alias* Constantinople/Istanbul. Like many other Scandinavians, he enlisted in the Byzantine empire's Varangian Guard, and rose to the rank of *sphatarokandidatos* (or colonel). The riches he amassed in Byzantium enabled him, on returning home, to buy the kingship of Norway jointly with his nephew, Magnus Olavsson.

Via Iceland and Greenland to America. By about the year 900, Olav the White's nephew, Harald Hårfagre (Harald Fairhair, or Finehair), had risen to power and unpopularity. Usually recognized as the first Norwegian monarch, he had enriched himself by depriving yeomen and freeholders of the rights of landownership and inheritance. These mostly prosperous families from western Norway preferred exile to oppression, and sailed off to settle in Iceland, with which many had long-standing ties. Olav the White's widow, Aud the Deep-eyed, was one of the first women to claim land in this Norwegian refuge and subsequent colony. (Her position precarious after the death of her son, Torstein the Red, she had sailed with his widow and their children, first to the Orkneys, thence to Iceland, accompanied by kinsmen from Ireland and the Hebrides.) Aud was instrumental in bringing Christianity to Iceland, where the Norwegian refugees soon established a democratic republic. Their *Althing* met annually at Thingvellir to pass laws and judgments: conceived to guarantee the people's rights and preclude tyranny, this parliament is the oldest in Europe.

In the early 980s one of the new Icelanders, Eric Thorvaldsson the Red, was sentenced by the Althing to three years' exile for an illegal (as opposed to a legitimate) killing. He went west in search of a land he had heard talk of. He found, and founded, Greenland (to which, in view of its ice and snow, he jokingly gave this name). His three years' exile over, he returned to Iceland in 985 and there persuaded 26 families to emigrate with him to Greenland. Only fourteen of their 25 boats completed the voyage, but this next phase of Norse colonization succeeded. Eric claimed land in the north-west, at the self-explanatory Eiriksfjord, and the kinsmen of his friend Herjolf settled and gave his name to Herjolfsnes in the south-west.

Delivering provisions to Herjolfsnes in 986, one Bjarni Herjolfsson was blown off course by storms, and returned to Iceland to report a new and unknown land. He was ridiculed for not having even gone ashore in what we now know to be America. In 1000 or thereabouts, however, Eric the Red's son Leif ('the Lucky') set sail with 34 men in Bjarni's old ship (a *knarr* or trading vessel). Reaching America, he found first a region which he called Helluland, 'Flatstone Land'. He next discovered a wooded country where forests reached to the sea, and named it Markland, meaning Woodland. Finally he went ashore amidst pleasant flat green fields, and named these Vinland ('Meadow' – or 'Vine' – Land). Here he built the now-famous *Leivsbuene* (Leif's Houses) at L'Anse aux Meadows in the well-named Newfoundland.

Eric's brother Thorvald followed, finding new lands further south. He may well have sailed as far as Florida, 'where the land turned'. He was killed by natives whom the Vikings knew as Skrelings. Being Christian, he was buried beneath two crosses on a site he had chosen for a Viking settlement: Krossnes, probably near Baltimore on the Chesapeake Bay.

The next expedition to Vinland was led by Thorfinn Karlsefni and his wife Gudrid (who had previously been married to Leif's brother Torstein). They brought three shiploads of Icelanders and cattle and stayed for several years, until attacks by the indigenous Indians forced them back to their boats.

Whilst in America, Gudrid gave birth to a son, Snorre, the first European born in the New World. He became the founding father of a great Icelandic family that included four bishops and the writer of sagas, Snorre Sturlasson. Ties with Vinland were not broken but maintained for several centuries, evidence being not only a small Norwegian coin from about 1090 found recently in Massachusetts, but also the mention in Church annals of Pope Pascal II's appointing a bishop to Vinland in 1121. By name Eric Upse, he is believed to have survived and may have returned safely to his native Iceland.

Before Christopher Columbus set sail so famously in 1492, he visited Iceland to investigate these earlier visits to Vinland. He travelled via Bristol in 1477, and in Reykjavik the Icelanders still know and show the house he occupied in the winter of that year.

Into Christianity. Having gained control of all of Norway – not in 872, as Norwegians are taught at school, but more probably fifteen-twenty years later – Harald Halvdansson Luva sat down and let his earl Ragnvald of Møre cut his hair (*luva* meaning hair, and Ragnvald being Rollo's father). Thanks to Ragnvald's blandishments, the king was from then on known as Hårfagre. This means Comely hair, but Fairhair or Finehair are more commonly used in English. Harald married fairly often, the term in many cases being euphemistic.

Ålesund, statue of Rollo/Gange Rolv

The Normans – whose influence and culture gradually ousted those of Norsemen, Danes and Anglo-Saxons in most of mainland Britain – were, in one ironical sense, vicarious Vikings. 'Norman', as in Normandy, derives very obviously from Norseman/Norwegian. Norse advances into north-west France are thought to have begun with one Rolf Ragnvaldsson. Better known as Rollo, Gangerolf or Gange Rolv (the *Gange* alluding in Norwegian to his being too tall for any horse), he is claimed as Danish by Danish historians and as Norwegian, and from Ålesund, by the citizens of Ålesund (where his statue now stands). It is however a moot point whether Rollo was ever even near Ålesund. His father had been made Earl of Møre, the surrounding province, by Harald Fairhair, but by then Rollo had probably been banished for pillaging in his own land. He is more likely to have grown up in the region of modern Hamar, and to have spoken the dialect of Hedmark, not of Møre.

Rollo spent his youth in the service of various Viking sea-kings before forming an army of Norsemen from Britain and Norway and sailing up the Seine in AD 911. The French king, Charles III ('the Simple'), placated the invader with a fief, a dukedom and the Treaty of Saint-Clair-sur-Epte.

Due to kiss ceremonially his sovereign's foot, as feudal custom required of a newly named duke, Rollo grabbed it instead and tipped Charles off the throne. The kingdom was his – a territory consisting of the modern départements of Seine Inférieure, Eure, Manche, Orne and Calvados, which for obvious reasons became known as *Normandie*. According to *The Vikings* by the Danish professor Brøndsted, the capital was Ruda or Rudaborg (the present-day Rouen), with place-names ending in *torp*, *tofte*, *gard* and *lond* being relics of Norse settlement. For the rest, the Norse tongue, whether the Møre or the Hedmark variety, soon vanished here almost without trace. Later dukes of Normandy included Rollo's great-great-grandson, William the Conqueror. As far as we know, Norwegian warriors took no further part in hostilities in Normandy until that fateful day, 6 June 1944.

Dying in 933 at the age of 80 (?), Harald was succeeded by his most notable (and probably eldest) son, Eric Bloodaxe. The latter's resolute and cunning queen, Gunnhild, was his cousin – and daughter of the last heathen king of Denmark, Gorm the Old. Eric's several sons succeeded in killing five of his brothers, until they were put to flight by the youngest and strongest, Håkon the Good.

Håkon lost his life in battle in AD 960, having long before lost the struggle against his subjects' pagan beliefs, such as sacrificing horses to the Norse gods. Eric Bloodaxe's eldest son followed, as King Harald II Gråfell. He ruled with the help of Eric's unruly brothers and unscrupulous mother, Queen Gunnhild. Her brother, Harald Bluetooth of Denmark, resented their independence and set his sights on Norway, inciting his earl there to oppose Gunnhild. The earl, Håkon Sigurdsson, murdered Harald Gråfell whilst on a visit to Denmark, then most of his brothers, and assumed power. Better known as the *Ladejarl* (Earl of Lade), he ruled Norway until 995 when he died, hiding in a pigsty from Olav Tryggvason, his throat cut by his serf.

Having, as his reward, murdered the serf, having served in England in the Danes' 'Great Army' (and, in Chester, wed the King of Dublin's daughter), this Olav Tryggvason named himself King Olav I. He had been christened in the Scilly Isles, and now set to evangelizing energetically. He built churches and appointed priests, but was to die a victim of his young wife's greed. After the princess from Dublin, he had married Tyra, whose father, Harald Bluetooth of Denmark, had been killed in battle by his own son, Svein. The last refused Olav the dowry due for Tyra, who insisted her husband sail south to claim it. Olav did so, in his *Ormen lange* (Long Snake), but was beset by fog and beaten by Svein's Swedish-Danish force. The remainder of his 720 men facing capture, Olav dived overboard and was never seen again (save in later legendary sightings in Jerusalem). All this, as every Norwegian knows, in the famous battle of Svolder – although no one has discovered where Svolder was.

Already king of Denmark, Svein (known as Forkbeard) was now also king of Norway. He was assisted by two sons of the Ladejarl, Eric and Svein who, no doubt mindful of their father's murder at Olav's bidding, had played a prominent part in the latter's defeat at Svolder.

King Canute of England was a son of Svein Forkbeard, and in 1015 summoned Eric to England. He left Norway in the care of Eric's infant son, Håkon – and the way clear for the next and most distinguished descendant of Harald Fairhair.

Olav Haraldsson, the later St Olav, is usually accredited with the conversion of Norway, both because of his life-work and the manner of his death. A short man, with brown hair and beard, he was dubbed Olav Digre, meaning Heavy set. As King Olav II, he ousted but spared the young earl Håkon, then proceeded to convert by the sword. 'You may not want to be Christian, but you shall', was his watchword. Those who resisted immediately lost their head. Having his Viking ships dragged up to Lake Mjøsa and rowed quietly under cover of darkness to Hamar, he in one night defeated a dozen provincial kings. In 1028, however, he was driven from Norway by England's king Canute. Olav counter-attacked two years later, but his ragtag army of exiles and fugitive criminals was no match for the opposing force of nobles and freeholders. On 29 July 1030 Olav was killed at Stiklestad, in Værdal north of Trondheim.

Stave churches.

The *stavkirker* that many regard as characteristically Scandinavian, and the finest examples of which survive in Norway, appear to have originated in Anglo-Saxon Britain. Evidence is the existence of a stave church at Greensted in Essex and the fact that Norway's first clergy came across from Northumbria and Ireland. As in 20th-century technology, innovations are often developed less by their inventors than by those who copy and adopt them. The Norsemen of the 11-12th centuries raised the stave church into an exquisite art form, which was first the subject of academic study by J. C. Dahl in 1837 and recently received the accolade of a magnificent volume in the UNESCO World Art series.

Origins and practicalities are uncomplicated. With forests abundant, staves were cut and planted in the soil at six-foot intervals. Larger trunks were sliced into planks affixed horizontally to the staves. A first inherent defect was the 'foundations': the buried part of the upright soon rotted naturally. For this reason those churches surviving from the 11th century – at Urnes in Norway, and Greensted – have been preserved by later trimming and reuse of the walling, with the uprights set in sill-beams and so raised off the ground. Thanks principally to this operation, 31 stave churches are still standing in Norway, out of an original total of around 750. The most striking survivals are at Borgund on the Sognefjord, at Hoprekstad, at Fantoft near Bergen and, likewise removed to a safe 'museum' site, at Bygdøy's Folkemuseum.

The initial, 11th-century plan was simple: rectangular nave, usually square chancel and sometimes aisles beside both. Vertical poles in the central nave served to heighten the roof. Elaboration came with the 13th century when stepped roofs became multiple, in the manner of a pagoda, and wood-carved ornamentation increased in intricacy. Animal-head finials projecting from roof-peaks and gables evoke gargoyles or the prows of Viking ships. The façades depict not only Christian scenes but also themes from Norse mythology. That the heathen-Christian confrontation should still have been fought out in late Viking stave churches fascinates scholars and laymen alike.

The Hoprekstad stave church, Vik

Olav Tryggvason, on a column in Trondheim, which he founded in AD 997

The Norse realm. After the battle of Stamford Bridge in 1066, which cost Norway not only King Harald Hardråde but also most of its nobles, their vanquisher, Harold Godwinson, had to force-march his Anglo-Saxon army south to face Duke William at Hastings. Thanks to *1066 and All That*, I need not repeat what happened there to Harold's eye, and England. Norsemen (of Norwegian, Danish and Norman French descent) inundated the country and left a lasting mark on its language, laws and customs.

The remnants of Harald Hardråde's army, defeated at Stamford Bridge, fled to the Orkneys. There Harald's second son, Olav, had also arrived safely with two sons of Tostig Godwinson, brother of the Anglo-Saxon king Harold (he of Hastings). The sons, Skule and Kjetil, were named by Olav *lendmen* (lendermen) of Norway, a title later changed to baron. From these sons of Tostig, and grandsons of Godwin of Wessex, tens of thousands of Norwegians descend – amongst them the writer of these lines.

When Olav returned to Norway, his brother Magnus (who had stayed to take care of the kingdom) gave him half, but on Magnus' death in 1069 the whole country became Olav's. Officially King Olav III, he was nicknamed Kyrre or Bonde. The latter means Farmer, the former Peaceful and is a commoner name for Olav and appropriate to his rule until 1093. The coin found in Massachusetts a few years ago, further proof that the Norsemen were still sailing to America well after Leif Eriksson's time, bore the head of Olav Kyrre.

Even in the days of Harald Fairhair, the Shetlands, Orkneys and Hebrides were firmly in Norwegian hands, ruled in the king's name by a *jarl* (or earl). One of the earliest on record was the elder brother of Rollo: one Einar, who was nicknamed Torveinar – Einar the Peat – because he taught the islanders to dig the bogs for this source of fuel. Olav III's son Magnus (*alias* Magnus Barefoot) is known to have visited Ireland on several occasions, and to have conquered the Isle of Man.

The illegitimate son that Magnus set to rule the island, Sigurd of Man, is better known (to Norwegians) as Sigurd Jorsalfar, the 'voyager to Jerusalem'. En route for the Holy Land, he undertook various gallant-charitable engagements such as ridding Mallorca of bandits, before going on to conquer Tyre and Sidon. When fellow crusaders failed to appear from England, France and Germany, he sailed to Byzantium, sold his ships to the emperor and rode his horse back to Norway. In the meantime, Norway had been ruled by his brothers Øystein and Olav. (The former is remembered for building hostels along many highways.)

The sexual prowess of their father, Magnus Barefoot, caused problems as time went by because unexpected sons and heirs would keep appearing. Some established their birthright by walking over glowing coals. Others did not. One, an Irishman called Gilchrist, was accepted as a true brother by 'Jerusalem' Sigurd after the death of brothers Olav and Øystein, but on condition he not claim the throne. When Sigurd died, however, to be succeeded by his son Magnus, Gilchrist lost no time in having Magnus deposed, blinded and castrated, and in seizing power as King Harald Gille Magnusson.

Norway's monarchy then split and drifted into illegitimacy. At one point the nation had three kings simultaneously, of whom only one had been born in wedlock: the crippled Inge Krokrygg (Hunchback). It was Inge who received the English cardinal, Nicholas Brakespeare, and accepted that Norway pay Peter's penny, symbolic allegiance to Rome.

Olav II was disinterred a year or so after his death at Stiklestad in 1030: his hair, beard and nails were found to have grown, his complexion was healthy and a fragrance exuded from the grave. Olav's personal bishop, the Englishman Grimkell, proposed a canonization which few opposed. Olav, 'the Eternal King', became Norway's patron saint. A spring appeared on the sandy spot where he had first been buried; it attracted mediaeval pilgrims, amongst whom the sick were necessarily cured. Since 1892 the site in Trondheim is marked by the altar of the rebuilt Nidaros Cathedral, erected *in memoriam* (and dedicated in Latin) to '*Olavus F. Haraldi*' and five other '*reges Norvegiæ* buried in this Cathedral church'.

Christianity in Norway was later considered to have started with the battle of Stiklestad. Conversion was however a gradual process, commencing some 50 years earlier under kings Håkon the Good and Olav Tryggvason, and completed 200 years later.

On the City Hall of Oslo, the capital he founded: Harald Hardråde ('Hardruler'), the last Viking king

(Nicholas founded the archbishopric of Nidaros and the bishopric of Hamar, before becoming Adrian IV, the only English pope.)

Norway was saved from a succession of bastard princes and a series of petty, crippling wars by the rise to power of a strong personality from Sunnhordland, south of Bergen. Erling Ormson Skakke belonged to an old and well-known family and was married to Christina, daughter of Sigurd 'Jerusalem' Jorsalfar. Returning from a crusade, Skakke had suffered a cut in the neck which kept him from holding his head straight. The people of Norway – whose history is lightened by the names they coin for those who make it – called him *Skakke*, Wryneck. At the battle of Veøy in the Romsdalfjord he defeated and succeeded Håkon II Herdebrei (Broadshoulders), a son of Inge the Hunchback's brother, Sigurd Munn (the Mouth). Skakke placed his young son Magnus on the throne, even having the archbishop (in return for vast concessions) crown him ceremonially – the first king of Norway to be so honoured. Having rid Norway of all pretenders true or false, and thus secured his son's future, Erling Skakke then gave his allegiance to the king of Denmark.

When son Magnus was a grown man, there arrived one day from the Faroes a stocky little priest called Sverre. He had been persuaded to take charge of the Birkebeiner (Birch-leg) Party, a poor and oppressed faction that was opposed to Magnus and had just lost its leader, Øystein Møyla ('Young girl'). Sverre's mother had told him that he was not the son of his accepted father (one Unas the Comb-maker) but of the sexually generous king Sigurd Munn – and thus brother of the Håkon Broadshoulders whom Skakke had recently killed.

At considerable cost the 'little man from the outer islands', as Sverre called himself, led the Birkebeiners to victory, first over Skakke and his barons at Kalvskinnet near Nidaros (Trondheim) in 1179 then, in 1184, over Skakke's son Magnus and the remaining barons at the naval battle of Fimreite in the Sognefjord. Nobility in Norway had been virtually eliminated – replaced by Sverre's partisans (for the most part) of the lowest social orders.

Sole ruler now of Norway, Sverre was nevertheless beset by problems, not only with Rome. This former dissident had also to contend with new dissident groups: the Øyskjeggene (the 'Bearded Ones from the islands') and, led by Bishop Arneson of Oslo, the Bagler (who took as their insignia, and for their name, the bishop's/shepherd's crook or *bagle*). Attacked on all fronts, and excommunicated, the Birkebeiner Sverre died peacefully in his bed in 1202.

His second son, Håkon III Sverresson, might well have succeeded in conciliating Rome and the warring factions had he not been poisoned (by Sverre's widow?) in 1204. While, in a short dynastic side-step, the son of a Birkebeiner chief was ruling as Inge Bårdsson, a young mother known in Norwegian history as Inga from Varteig announced that her son Håkon had been sired by King Håkon III. She proved her case by walking over burning coals. The Baglers, alarmed by this apparent link with legitimacy, set out to suppress it, but two Birkebeiners carried the baby to safety, skiing over the mountains from what later became Lillehammer to Rena in Østerdal. The little prince Håkon later reached Nidaros unharmed, where Inge Bårdsson cared for and educated him at court and at the cathedral school. He was named crown prince, to the detriment and chagrin of Inge's brother Skule, and succeeded Inge on his death in 1217, Skule becoming his regent.

Håkon IV Håkonsson was to rule well. He restored the ancient kingdom's fortunes, making its power felt again in Iceland, Greenland and the other island-earldoms to the west. Håkon married one illegitimate daughter to King Harald of Man, who in return accepted allegiance. Harald may have gained a wife but he lost his sovereignty – and his life: while the royal newly-weds were sailing home to Man from a magnificent marriage in Bergen, their ship, a wedding-present, sank with all hands in a storm. Another daughter, Christina, married the second son of King Alfonso of Spain. Håkon sent ambassadors to all of the then-known world with fitting gifts for his fellow monarchs – usually well-trained hunting hawks from his falconry in Bergen. He even had an ambassador accompany a polar-bear cub to the caliph of Baghdad. In his capital of Bjørgvin (Bergen) Håkon IV built beautiful churches and the hall that bears his name, Håkonshallen.

The resentment of Skule, King Inge's brother and Håkon's former regent, continued to fester. Though Håkon had married his daughter Margaret, honoured him with a dukedom and ceded him one third of the kingdom, Skule rebelled. He named as his earl in Iceland the famous writer of sagas, Snorre Sturlasson. Inevitably, once Håkon had had Skule and his son killed, at the monastery of Elgeseter near Nidaros, Snorre had to die too – at the hands of Håkon's henchmen whilst sitting in the sauna at his farm of Reykholt.

Håkon himself (who had even aspired to be Holy Roman Emperor) died in 1263 at Kirkwall in the Orkneys. Commanding an immense fleet on a naval campaign, he caught pneumonia and died after a small skirmish that the Scots like to call the Battle of Largs.

The Birkebeiner partisans Torstein Skjevla and Skjervald Skrukka escaping, on skis, from the Bagler faction with the future King Håkon IV

Håkon IV and Margaret's first son died young; their second son lived only just long enough to assume power, and his son succumbed at the age of 27. That left the royal couple's third son to become king as Magnus VI, *alias* Lagabøter (the Lawmender). He not only justified this title but also reformed Norway's hierarchy, aligning the ancient *lendmen*, *skutil-sveiner* and *kjertesveiner* with the *baroner* (barons), *riddere* (knights) and *væpnere* (squires) used elsewhere in Europe. Magnus VI is remembered (by some) for having dismantled the strong and prestigious Norse realm which his father had worked to revive.

After Magnus' death in 1280, power was shared between his younger son Håkon and elder son Eric (later named *Prestehater*, Hater of priests). Eric's daughter Margaret (granddaughter of the Scottish king Alexander III) was the 'Maid from Norway' sent to England to marry Edward II, but who got lost on the way. Eric died in 1299, leaving Håkon to rule alone.

Håkon V was an able man, talented, and considered so good a Christian that many later wanted him made a saint. Saintly behaviour did not prevent him siring a natural daughter, Agnes, the ancestor of many leading families in Norway. Oslo especially remembers Håkon V for having transferred the capital there from Bjørgvin/Bergen, and constructed at Akersnes the castle that became the fortress and palace of Akershus. He was crowned king in Oslo in 1299.

Håkon's only legitimate daughter, Ingebjørg, wed the Swedish king Eric and bore him a son, Magnus. Marrying Blanca of Namur, this Magnus VII was king when the Black Death struck. In Norway, never heavily peopled, the plague took a terrible toll. Estimates of losses vary from 50% to 67% of the population, which after 1349 numbered no more than 225,000. Of the kingdom's 270 knights, 200 succumbed. In Nidaros alone, only 40 of the bishopric's 300 priests survived. Whole regions were emptied, farms abandoned. On the royal estate of Framstad near the present-day Gjøvik were found only skeletons – and so many mice that the place was renamed Mustad, Mouse Farm.

The Black Death dealt Norway such a blow that, in a sense, the nation's back was broken. Lacking spiritual and lay leaders, its army depleted and its economy shattered, it became to a greater or lesser extent an impoverished pawn to its stronger neighbours – for the duration of the '400-year-long night'.

Prior to the catastrophe, Magnus VII had arranged for his youngest son Håkon to succeed him, which he did at the age of fifteen in 1355. Four years later, this Håkon VI was betrothed to Margaret, the six-year-old daughter of the Danish king Valdemar Atterdag. In 1363 they were married in Copenhagen and became Norway's new royal couple, the queen now all of ten years old.

Young Margaret often sat alone, cold and hungry in Akershus Castle. She would write pathetic letters to her husband in Copenhagen, begging him to arrange credit with some local merchant so that she and her little court should not starve or freeze to death. A son was born to her, and named Olav in memory of his illustrious forebear.

This prince became Norway's king Olav IV or V (we have not lost count: historians differ) upon the death of his father Håkon VI (who, in a 19th-century recount, became Håkon VIII). Olav's reign was short; his mother Margaret however soldiered on, extending her sway slowly over Scandinavia. Historians do not question her competence, nor that the peoples of Norway, Sweden and Denmark thrived in her time. Although running counter to strict laws of succession, the Norwegian state council in 1388 named Margaret 'Norges rikes mektige frue og rette husbonde', 'The realm of Norway's mighty lady and true husband'. The entire nobility, led by the archbishop of Nidaros, recognized her sovereign for life, and founder of a new royal line.

In Sweden Margaret's rival, Albrecht of Mecklenburg, ridiculed her as the 'trouserless king' but his own nobles, in 1388, recognized to her the same rights and titles as Norway, and in the following year Albrecht renounced his claim to Sweden. Once the city of Stockholm had submitted, in 1398, every Nordic land was in Margaret's capable hands.

The death of her only son created a problem of succession. The only heir apparent was an infant great-nephew, Eric of Pomerania. In 1397, after lengthy discussions to which no Norwegian bishop was invited, the very first Nordic Council voted in the Kalmar Union – of Scandinavia or Norden as it was then called. The fifteen-year-old Eric became its first 'triple king', and Copenhagen his capital.

Great-aunt Margaret kept a tight hand on the reins, even after Eric came of age in 1400. Whenever, for example, he visited Norway – four times in all after 1388 – he received from her detailed marching orders. Norway's 'true husband' left nothing to chance, ruling with intelligence and skill until her death, aged almost 60, in 1412.

When Margaret died King Eric was 30 years old. Athletic and handsome, his contemporary image was that of the parfit knight. But behind this comely exterior lay a violent temperament. Eric was often unable to contain his rage, especially once death had deprived him of

Margaret's restraining hand. This we know from his correspondence – disrespectful even to the Pope. Both historians and historical novelists seem, for some strange reason, to have neglected this remarkable monarch: his peculiar mentality and long vicissitudinous life; his struggle against the Hanseatic towns of northern Germany and his own nobles; his magnificent, even extravagant pilgrimage to Jerusalem; his long war in Holstein and (backed by the fire-power of his new fortress at Kronborg) his revolutionary imposition of a maritime toll on all ships passing through Danish waters.

Dissatisfaction closed in on Eric: uprisings were led by Engelbrekt Engelbrektsson in Sweden, and in Norway by the nobleman Amund Sigurdsson Bolt. The latter however made his peace with the Norwegian state council, which in 1436 quelled another insurrection under the farmer Halvor Gråtopp (Greytop).

Norway, at least, remained to Eric when in 1438 the Danish and Swedish state councils severed their allegiance. Living in Gotland, partly by piracy, Eric was attacked in 1449 by the Swedish king, Karl Knutsson Bonde; surrendering Gotland to Denmark and its new King Christian, Eric returned to his native Pomerania where, at 77 years, his adventurous life ended in 1459.

Eric's English wife, Philippa, had died childless in 1412 (the king thereafter living with his mistress, Cecilia, until his death). Lacking a legitimate heir, he wanted his cousin, Bogislaus of Pomerania, accepted as successor. The Norwegian state council acquiesced, those of Sweden and Denmark refused, and the last in 1439 elected instead Eric's nephew Christopher, of the Wittelsbach family, former rulers of Bavaria.

The Swedes and Danes prevailed. In 1442 Christopher of Bavaria was crowned king in Oslo. Popular in Norway, he co-operated with the state council, handled well the problem of Hanseatic Bergen and kept Scandinavia's Kalmar Union, however precariously, intact. But his rule lasted only five years: in 1447 he died at the age of 30, leaving an eighteen-year-old widow, Dorothea of Brandenburg.

The '400-year-long Night'.

Many believe that Norway was conquered and ruled forcibly by Denmark. The fact is that the question of succession within the Kalmar Union was so frequent and intractable a problem as to exclude the possibility of peaceful and equitable joint rule. After the death of Christopher of Bavaria, all three state councils sought a successor. One claimant was Christian, the unmarried son of a minor German count who arrived from Oldenburg and, so they say, was accepted as the Nordic monarch because of being willing to marry the late king's widow. A second, simultaneous 'king of Norway' was the Swede Karl Knutsson Bonde. The Norwegian state council had in fact promised Christian the throne, but the archbishop of Nidaros/Trondheim so disliked the Danish commander-in-chief in Norway that, in preference to the German monarch, he invited Karl Knutsson to Nidaros and crowned him king in 1449.

In order to precipitate a show-down, Christian moved Danish troops into Sweden. With the bulk of Norway also backing Christian, Karl finally modified his claims. He proposed, with rather transparent pragmatism, that whichever of the two survived the other should take all. Christian, seventeen years younger, saw no reason to refuse. As even the Swedes later rejected Karl, Christian came to rule all three

Nordic states, and even Finland. With the help of his (and his predecessor's) Queen Dorothea, he founded a dynasty that was to reign over Norway and Denmark for the following four centuries.

Christian sailed north to Nidaros and was crowned with great pomp and ceremony in the cathedral there in 1450: Norway's '400-årsnatten', the '400-year-long night' of Danish occupation, had begun.

Incompetent in financial matters and continually embroiled in wars and disputes, Christian I was dubbed the 'bottomless purse' by his Swedish subjects – who deposed him in 1464. Karl Knutsson was recalled in lieu, but died in 1470. Christian's attempts to regain power were thwarted by the Swedish viceroy at the battle of Brunkeberg in 1471.

Two years earlier, Christian had married his only daughter to the king of Scotland, James, for a dowry of 60,000 gold coins. Bankrupt again after Brunkeberg, Christian pawned the Shetlands and Orkneys to his royal Scottish son-in-law – a surety which, some Norwegians recall, is still not redeemed to this day. (Strictly speaking, Christian's pawning the islands without the consent of the Norwegian state council was illegal, since they belonged not to Denmark but Norway.)

Christian I visited Norway just five times in the course of his long reign, sending instead the most unlikely and intransigent bureaucrats. The archbishop of Nidaros, Aslak Bolt, had died before Christian's coronation there in 1450 and, in defiance of Rome, the king replaced him with a German adventurer, Marcellus di Niiverus.

Disliked equally by the Pope and his own subjects, Christian died in 1481. His eldest son, Hans, was crowned king of Norway in Nidaros Cathedral in 1483, his queen the pious, twenty-year-old Christine of Saxony.

Wars without and wretched conditions within also marked the reign of this reputedly nonchalant monarch. A Swedish-Norwegian nobleman, Knut Alvsson Tre Rosor (Three Roses), led an insurrection but was treacherously murdered – despite his white flag of truce – whilst defending Akershus Castle against loyalist troops. King Hans slowly improved as a ruler, though given to fits of temper during which his judgment suffered. Having named his son Christian viceroy in 1506, he died at Ålborg in 1513.

Christian II was to be Norway's last Catholic king. His queen was Isabella of Habsburg, sister of the famed Charles V of Spain (but called by her Norwegian subjects Elisabet). As a young duke in Bergen, Christian had fallen in love with Dyveke Willums, the daughter of a Dutch innkeeper. He kept up the liaison after marrying Elisabet and becoming king: his subjects were outraged – and later writers provided with yet another titillating episode in Norway's royal history.

Christian II was crowned king of Norway in 1514 in Oslo (which notwithstanding was not yet renamed Christiania) and king of Denmark one year later in Copenhagen. He is probably remembered best as author of the 'Stockholm Bloodbath'. Having defeated their army in 1520, Christian persuaded the leaders of Sweden to accept him as their hereditary king – by dint of executing 82 of their number. The survivors, understandably, dubbed him 'Christian Tyrann'.

Despised by the Swedes, he was liked by Norwegians, despite his reputation for fecklessness and dishonesty. He continued the practice started by his grandfather of importing Danish bureaucrats, and opposed the power of the Church. The Danes' hatred was none the

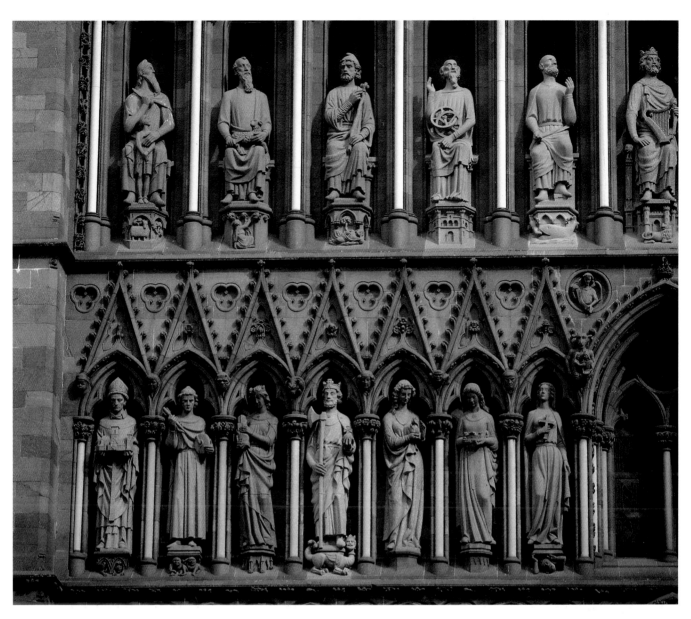

Trondheim, façade of the Nidaros Cathedral

less such that an uprising against him succeeded: its leader, one Duke Frederick, became king and Christian was exiled – to the Netherlands home of his faithful mistress, Dyveke. With the help of the emperor, Charles V of Spain, Christian sailed for Norway in 1531. Over 4000 of his men were lost in the difficult sea-crossing and the 2–3000 survivors failed to take Akershus Castle (in common with every other assailant before or since). Christian finally surrendered, having been promised a safe passage to his uncle in Copenhagen, the new Danish king, Frederick I. The latter, however, imprisoned him on arrival and left him incarcerated for 27 years until his death in 1559.

Though brother of Norway's former King Hans, Frederick I proved to be very different. He stripped the (Catholic) archbishop of Nidaros of his fiefdom of Trondheim, prevented Denmark's bishops from suppressing the Lutherans, and gave their fellows in Schleswig religious freedom. This last was a perhaps predictable act, since Frederick's son and heir, the future Christian III, was already the acknowledged head of Denmark's Lutheran movement. In retaliation, Archbishop Olav of Nidaros postponed Frederick's coronation indefinitely, with the result that the king was never crowned.

The struggle between entrenched Catholicism and the Protestantism spreading from Lutheran Germany became a momentary leitmotiv of Nordic history. Frederick's choice of heir, his son Christian, was opposed by the state councils of both Norway and Denmark (Christian being staunchly Protestant; as a young man he had, in 1521, been present at the 'diet of Worms' in which Martin Luther defended his doctrine). And on Frederick's death in 1533 the Danish state council proclaimed his second son, the twelve-year-old Hans. It was however obliged to acknowledge Christian in 1534, as a result of the *Grevefeide*, the Struggle of the Counts. Resistance continued in the provinces, and only in 1536 was Copenhagen, and with it both kingdoms, fully under Christian's control.

Crowned in Copenhagen in 1537, as King Christian III of Denmark and Norway, he considered the latter too insignificant to rank as a kingdom in its own right. He declared it subject to Denmark 'in perpetuity'. Norway's bishops were imprisoned, silenced or exiled; the Norwegian state council was dismissed; the '400-year-long night' grew even darker.

With the help of his barons and bureaucrats in Norway, Christian proceeded to confiscate the wealth amassed through the ages by the Catholic church. The churches themselves were stripped of their precious relics, their gold and silver taken to line Christian's coffers. Priests were 'converted', like Nordic Vicars of Bray, or replaced by 'right-thinking' laymen, and 'superintendents' substituted for bishops. Many bishoprics were without either for quite some time, although Catholic priests who kept a low profile and acted neutrally stayed put.

After the removal of their state council in 1537, Norwegians were given the so-called *Herredager* ('Days' or 'Assemblies of the Lords') in which issues could be raised and judged. (After a farmers' revolt in Telemark, for example, five death sentences were handed down by one such ad hoc tribunal.) Trade flourished (even if the profits went mostly to German and Danish merchants) and, by the time he died on New Year's Day 1559, Christian III had turned his realm's economy round from a deficit of a half-million thaler to reserves of 100,000 thaler.

Christian IV followed, all of eleven years old when in 1588 his short-lived (if fast-living) father, Frederick II, died of drink. Christian's popularity with Norwegians is indicated by their giving him, like the heroes of the Viking era, a nickname – 'Christian Quart' or '*Kvarten*' – and explained no doubt by the frequency and pomp of his visits to their country. The first of the 30-odd royal tours, in June 1591, was marked by 'the greatest party ever given in Norway'. First, in Oslo, Christian was welcomed by the *stender* at Akershus Castle. Then in every parish the sheriff and two leading councillors came out, with the local nobility and burghers (often more than 1000), to welcome and pay homage to the young king. A sumptuous meal followed, some throwing themselves off grandstands to seize a piece of the costly red cloth that had covered the royal dais.

Christian IV was crowned in a magnificent ceremony in Copenhagen in 1596. His rule was very long – almost 60 years – and dominated by the Thirty Years' War (1618-48). The Lutheran alliance appointed him *Oberst* (supreme commander) and as such he repeatedly joined battle with General Tilly and Wallenstein. The latter occupied all of Jutland, the largest of Christian's Danish possessions, but when the emperor disclosed plans to allot that province to Catholic Spain, Christian won in negotiation what he had lost in war.

Frederick, Duke of Schleswig-Holstein, succeeded his unloved father, Christian III. Opposed to his religiosity, Frederick II disregarded his father for years, refusing to see him even on his deathbed. Disregarding the state council also, he raised an army to conquer, and annex, the troublesome German province of Ditmarsken. He faced on his return a confrontation with an irate state council, but in 1559 was none the less crowned king of Denmark and Norway, at the age of 25.

Relations deteriorated equally with his cousin, the newly crowned Eric XIV of Sweden. Both were rivals for the hand of Mary Stuart – both in vain – and Frederick was to reach the ripe age of 38 before finding a bride, his fifteen-year-old cousin, Elisabeth of Mecklenburg.

Lands as well as love were the subject of Eric and Frederick's rivalry. While Eric of Sweden aspired to rule Norway,

Thanks to his regular visits, Christian was well known and loved in Norway and knew and loved it well. He sailed north as far as Vardø (under the alias of 'Captain Christian Frederiksen'). He established Kongsberg, Røros and Christiansand and, fascinated by mining, developed the first's silver-works. His drinking bouts in Bergen left a lasting impression on that city. The attention Christian paid to Oslo was rather more edifying: visiting the city immediately after the great fire of 1624, he took part, a keen architect, in its replanning. Relocated around Akershus Castle, it was renamed in his honour Christiania.

Saddened in old age by the death of his son, Prince Christian (whom many mistook for the king's twin brother), Christian Quart died in his bed in 1648. In 1988 Scandinavians fondly celebrated the 400th anniversary of the birth of this well-loved king – who in fact lost every battle he fought (as well as one eye), made countless women pregnant and drank anything alcoholic in legendary amounts.

Christian IV left a great number of children – most born out of wedlock. With no legitimate son surviving, the next in line was Frederick, a feckless north German prince who had lost most of the provinces given him by his father. He was nevertheless well educated, and especially interested in politics, history and natural science. He curbed the influence of the nobles and other classes in his own territories, and in 1643 married Sophie Amalia of Brunswick-Lüneburg. As a bachelor Frederick had fathered one son – the future Count Ulrick Frederick Gyldenløve – but he made a faithful husband and the six children given him by his energetic queen were unquestionably blue-blooded.

Though apprehensive of the independence and forcefulness of their intended ruler, the Danish nobility accepted Frederick, who in July 1648 was honoured by the Danish *stender*. He then set sail for Norway and was proclaimed at Akershus in the presence of 712 delegates (and – as recent excavations have revealed – at a cost of 16,000 wine-glasses; breaking one's glass is the customary conclusion of a *Skål* or toast).

Frederick III never again visited Norway, but in 1664 sent there as governor-general his clever, charming (and illegitimate) son, Count Ulrick Frederick Gyldenløve. Famed throughout Europe as a general of the Holy Roman Empire and grandee of Spain (and in Scandinavia as commander-in-chief of the Swedish campaign of 1657-60), Gyldenløve ('Golden Lion') was popular in Norway. He lived in the town of Larvik and carved out the territory that later became the province of the counts of Laurvig. Building a fleet of ships for coastal defence, he also laid the foundations of a Norwegian navy.

After Frederick III's death in 1670, the twin kingdoms of Norway and Denmark fell to his son, Christian V. Fathering children was one of the few things this weak and debauched ruler could manage, totalling seven with his queen, Charlotte Amalia of Hessen-Cassel, and five with his official mistress, Sophie Amalia Moth. At his coronation Christian himself placed crowns on his head and the queen's, to demonstrate who was in charge (and perhaps inspire Napoleon?). His chief minister was an enterprising German by the name of Peter Schuhmacher. Created Count Griffenfeld (by which name he is better known), he in time appropriated much of the royal power. He was finally disgraced and condemned to death, and his seat of Jarlsberg near Tønsberg allocated to the Wedel family who own it still. His sentence commuted to life imprisonment, Count Griffenfeld spent the rest of his days in the odd octagonal bastion on Munkholmen, a five-minute ferry ride from Trondheim.

Frederick aimed to annex Sweden. Their armies advanced and retreated repeatedly until a peace treaty was signed finally in 1570.

Frederick II visited Norway only once, but appointed a governor to Akershus whose assignment was to protect the farmers and peasants from exploitation by Danish officialdom. The last years of Frederick's reign were peaceable, and marked by improved economic conditions – in Norway as well as Denmark. Frederick developed a sizeable Danish-Norwegian navy in which many Norwegians served. He had less success in his attempts to conscript Norway's farmers into his army.

Christian V's fortifications at Fredrikstad

Christian V visited Norway twice and, happily for the Norwegians, left the running of their country to his older half-brother, Gyldenløve. The king himself is remembered in Norway for the *Norske Lov* ('Christian V's Norwegian Law'), parts of which remained drafted in Dutch until the present century.

Dying in 1699, Christian V was succeeded by his son, Frederick IV, aged 28, married to Louise of Mecklenburg and already a confirmed bigamist. (He later added to this an adulterous affair with Countess Anna Sophia Reventlow.) Despite his lack of education, Frederick IV matured with time into a competent statesman and worthy king. He enjoyed good relations with his subjects, his Norwegian 'children' (whom he visited in 1704 and 1709) looking on him as 'their father in Copenhagen'.

Russia was at the time being 'brought into Europe' and transformed, from mediaeval to relatively modern, by Peter the Great. He was on good terms with Norway's King Frederick, but the relationship floundered when the latter refused to let his elder son marry the tsar's eldest daughter. This Princess Anna married instead his worst rival, the Duke of Holsten-Gottorp. The resulting son, called initially Count of Kiel, was to become Tsar Peter III – and the predictable source of considerable trouble for the twin kingdoms.

In later life Frederick worked to foster the education he himself lacked, building 240 schools on his various estates and sending missionaries, among them Thomas von Westen, to the eskimos in Greenland.

Frederick IV died in 1730, to be followed by his very dissimilar son, Christian VI. Sombre and pious, Christian was the only son of the 'legitimate' queen, Louise. He was not alone in his outrage at his father's living with Anna Reventlow as his queen whilst still married to Louise. That all six children Anna bore him should die was considered divine retribution.

Piety was the keynote of Christian's life and reign. He was short, shy and introverted and had, in Sophie Magdalena of Culmbach-Bayreuth, made a good match. They had three children and stayed faithfully and joylessly together, recluses until the king died in 1746 – 47 years old. He had reintroduced serfdom for the peasants and banned anything that smacked of theatre or such worldly entertainment. He did however make the care of vagrants and needy people compulsory, so his rule might be said to have benefitted some.

The moral laxity repugned by Frederick IV's son, Christian, returned with his grandson, Frederick V. Establishing his prowess not in matters of state but in bed, he proved as usual very popular with his northern subjects. That popularity peaked when, after a remarkably carnal bachelorhood, Frederick married the English princess Louise, daughter of George II. When Louise died giving birth to their sixth child in 1751, the court arranged a hasty wedding with Juliana-Marie of Brunswick. Though chronically drunk, the rewed king managed one son. Unaffected by his alcoholism, his twice breaking a leg whilst drunk and his stumbling around Copenhagen accompanied by loose women, Frederick's popularity with the Norwegians was put to the test, and proven, in 1758-62. His dukedoms of Schleswig and Holstein menaced by the rival Count of Kiel (the future Tsar Peter III), the Norwegians rallied, volunteers and conscripts streaming south. In all, 16,000 Norwegian foot-soldiers set out to engage Peter's army of 80,000, for the most part cavalry.

Frederick's marshal was the French general Saint-Germain, who marched boldly into Mecklenburg on a broad front. The Russians had however vanished, leaving the Norwegian advance party somewhat non-plussed. It transpired that in the meantime the tsarina had imprisoned her husband and seized power. Catherine II thus spared the twin kingdoms a costly war (though some 3250 demobilized Norwegians died of disease trying to find their way home).

The monarchy, rather tarnished by Frederick V's shaky reign, worsened under his successor from debauched to demented. Aged seventeen when his father died in 1766, Christian VII was (like later his English contemporary, George III) mentally ill. He remained so, on and off, for the 42 years of his reign. The English princess, Caroline Mathilda whom he married at the age of fifteen, he was later to abandon and mistreat – a royal non-romance that is the subject of several studies and historical novels. The king consorted with prostitutes and drunkards, and sacked ministers at whim, but could also be courteous and conduct receptions in strict accordance with the protocol of the age. He travelled round Europe with a large entourage, smashed furniture, ranted and raged, but at other times behaved impeccably. The Dutch in particular have reason to remember the state visit of young Christian VII: chief minister Count Bernstorff did his best to cover up the scandals but was soon relieved of his duties. His replacement was the king's surgeon, a German named Johann Friedrich Struensee. He rose rapidly (even making poor Queen Caroline pregnant in 1771) and was soon effectively master of Denmark and Norway. Count Struensee's fall from power was equally conclusive: worsted by the king's brother in 1771, he was tried and executed the following year.

Perhaps because of this peculiar political climate, a sense of national identity was aroused amongst Norwegians. The activity that this new national consciousness prompted was to culminate in the events at Eidsvoll in 1814. Already in 1772 a Norwegian Literary Society had been founded in Copenhagen by Ole Gjerløw Meyer. Its best-known members were the poet Johan Herman Wessel and the bishop-to-be, Johan Nordahl Brun.

On 14 April 1784 there occurred in Copenhagen something rather unexpected. Christian VII's son and heir, Frederick, who was sixteen years old and had just been confirmed, led a successful coup d'état. The king's half-brother tried to prevent the take-over but the young prince had his almost comatose father sign the necessary papers. Prince Frederick and his associates, counts Bernstorff and Stampe, were to introduce radical reforms such as freedom of the press, medical services throughout the two kingdoms and a modernization of criminal law.

In 1788 took place the so-called Cranberry War. In a combined operation with Russia against Sweden, a Danish-Norwegian army marched into the now-Swedish province of Båhuslen and threatened Gothenburg. The army was however poorly equipped and supplied, and expected to live off the land (which, yielding only *tyttebær* – cranberries, gave the war its name). Though victorious, hundreds of home-bound Norwegian troops died of malnutrition and disease.

On the death of his father, 'mad King Christian', Frederick VI in 1808 assumed de jure the powers he had exercised de facto during his father's long alienation. Frederick had married, while still heir apparent in 1790, a daughter of Prince Karl of Hessen, Norway's commander-in-chief during the Cranberry War. The couple had eight children but, with only two daughters surviving infancy, the royal line was to die out with Frederick.

The first decade of the 19th century saw Scandinavia embroiled in wars within wars. Frederick's staunch support of Bonaparte involved the northern kingdoms inevitably in the Napoleonic Wars. In 1801, under Nelson, the Royal Navy sailed into Copenhagen and, to prevent its use by Frederick's French allies, put paid to the Danish-Norwegian fleet. (The first ship into battle, the 54-gun *Glatton*, was commanded by Captain 'Bounty' Bligh.) The Navy then went on (as in World War II) to blockade Norway, and the deprivations his compatriots suffered are movingly rendered in Henrik Ibsen's famous poem *Terje Vigen*. The naval blockade made Danish administration of Norway difficult, and King Frederick in Copenhagen was in any case preoccupied with the larger European scene. A government commission was given wide powers to rule Norway, and Prince Christian August of Augustenburg appointed viceroy and commander-in-chief. Under this outstanding leader (whom his men called 'the Gustenborger') the Norwegians easily routed the invading army that Sweden, attacked by Russia and Denmark, sent against them in 1808.

By 1809 Sweden had to sue for peace, a peace that again allowed of sufficient prosperity for Frederick to found, in 1811, the Oslo university that bore his name. In 1813 he appointed to Norway a new governor-general, his charming 27-year-old cousin who was to become, after Eidsvoll, King Christian Frederick.

In Sweden, the ageing Carl XIII had no heir and – forgetting their defeat at his hands in 1808? – the Swedes invited the Gustenborger to become crown prince of Sweden. A reply was made unnecessary by his dying in 1810, whereupon a Swedish delegation was sent to enlist in lieu Napoleon's marshal, Bernadotte. The son of a French lawyer and later ennobled as Prince of Pontecorvo, Jean-Baptiste Bernadotte accepted. By name now Crown Prince Carl Johan, he was soon master of Sweden.

In 1809 Sweden had ceded Finland to Russia. When Napoleon was defeated in 1814, the victorious powers (in the Treaty of Kiel) supported their ally Bernadotte's claim to Norway in compensation, and coerced Frederick VI in Copenhagen to accept. After centuries of see-saw warring with Sweden, it was scarcely to be expected that the Norwegians would take kindly to this sudden, unconsulted imposition of Swedish rule. On 9 April 1814 – a momentous date in Norway's history – 112 representatives of the towns, provinces and armed forces met at Eidsvoll, in the home of Carsten Anker, and determined on an independent constitution for their country. Taking the constitutions of France and the young United States as their model, the 'men of Eidsvoll' worked for almost six weeks. By 17 May 1814 the new constitution was ready for signing – by the new hereditary monarch, Christian Frederick. Statues now at Eidsvoll commemorate this milestone in Norway's history. Count Wedel, Christian Magnus Falsen, Wilhelm F. K. Christie and Nicolai Wergeland are some of the leaders Norwegians recall with pride for this courageous initiative.

The reaction of the great powers was predictable. With their backing, Bernadotte moved into Norway on a broad front. The Norwegian army, performing less impressively than its politicians, was easily defeated in the autumn of 1814. Young Christian Frederick abdicated – later to mount the throne of Denmark as Christian VIII (and to sire, out of wedlock, the writer of fairy-tales, Hans Christian Andersen – though this may itself be a fairy-tale).

On 20 October 1814 a new Norwegian parliament met and approved union with Sweden. Old King Carl XIII of Sweden became Carl (or rather Karl) II of Norway – the latter's Karl I having been the (equally Swedish) Karl Knutsson Bonde. (As with James I/VI of England/Scotland, Swedes

The Eidsvoll Building (above),
Carsten Anker (left) and
Henrik Wergeland (below)

insist on calling Karl II of Norway 'Carl/Karl XIII'.) The regal discrepancy was not resolved by Carl's dying in 1818 (having never visited Norway) and Bernadotte's succession as Carl XIV/III of Sweden and Norway.

For those present-day Norwegians or their parents who have endured defeat in war and enemy occupation, it may seem strange that Bernadotte, a king forced upon a defeated Norway, should in time have become popular, even loved. He left Norwegians their Storting ('Great Thing' viz. parliament) and many institutions that are the marks of national independence (although foreign relations remained firmly in his hands). A lover of liberty like the patriotic poet Henrik Wergeland wrote in honour of Bernadotte who, closing his eyes in 1844 at the age of 81, was widely mourned. Under his guidance, culture had thrived in both Norway and Sweden. Most historians agree that he ruled wisely, but that the true foundations of Norway's developing democracy were the '17 May king', Christian Frederick, and the constitution of Eidsvoll.

Bernadotte and his popular Queen Désirée (or Desideria as she was known in Sweden) had a son before acceding to the throne, to which the boy succeeded as King Oscar I. (He was born in 1799 and at an early age already spoke perfect Swedish. When his father addressed the Storting in November 1814, the fifteen-year-old prince read the Swedish translation impeccably.) Oscar was more introverted than his father, Bernadotte, but he and Josephine, his French-born queen, soon won Norwegian hearts. Oscar revived Norway's political and cultural life. Business boomed, new industries were established and shipping increased in importance. The royal palace in Christiania was completed by architect Linstow during Oscar's reign. The king was an active factor in Denmark's war with Germany in 1848, and planned to extend his rule over the rest of Scandinavia. In this he was however thwarted by ill-health and, when he died in 1859 at the age of 60, his son Karl had for quite some time been in effective command of the country.

The latter's coronation in Nidaros Cathedral – as Karl IV of Norway/Carl XV of Sweden – was a magnificent occasion, immortalized not only in Aasmund Olavsson Vinje's poem *Færdaminne*, 'Memories from a Journey'. Handsome, extroverted and a fine horseman, the popular new king reminded the two peoples more of his grandfather, Bernadotte, than of his more reserved father. Karl IV was noted for his remarkable (and reciprocal) success with women – wed, unwed or widowed: a number of prominent families in both Sweden and Norway claim him as a forebear.

As crown prince, Karl had on several occasions acted as viceroy in Norway. He was obviously fond of the Norwegians – and their wives – and promised to abolish the unpopular office of governor-general, which Norwegians regarded as discriminatory and symbolic of their subservient status. Shortly before Christmas in 1859, the Storting removed from the constitution all mention of a governor-general, but the Swedes' reaction was such that Karl was forced to reincorporate the relevant clauses. The Norwegians were outraged, and relations soured between the two peoples.

Karl suffered another set-back in 1864. Denmark and Germany having resumed hostilities, he promised to help Copenhagen by sending troops from Sweden and Norway. Their respective parliaments however – the Riksdag in Stockholm and the Storting in Christiania – repudiated the promise: Denmark, unaided, was defeated. Karl's daughter Louise was married to the eldest son of the Danish king, Christian IX (the 'Father-

Holmenkollen, Oslo: statue of the late King Olav V who, as the nineteen-year-old crown prince, was junior ski-jump champion here in 1922

in-Law of Europe'): Karl's political humiliation was also a family affair.

Karl IV's only son by his Dutch queen, Louise, died in infancy and, when the 46-year-old king himself passed away in 1872, his younger brother succeeded as Oscar II. Oscar was a competent person, well suited for high office. He spent considerable time in Norway, showing interest in the Folkemuseum and financing other museums. The stuffed lion in the Tøyen zoological museum was donated by him. In weightier matters of state, however, Oscar saw relations with his Norwegian subjects take an inevitable turn for the worse. In Christiania, the reimposition of a governor-general still rankled; in view of their increasing foreign trade and superior merchant fleet, Norwegians also demanded an autonomous consular service; the 'personal union' forced on Norway by the great powers in 1814 was generally considered there to have outlived its usefulness. The breach with Sweden was formalized in 1905 when the Norwegian prime minister, Christian Michelsen, declared that 'because of unparliamentary behaviour, Oscar II had ceased to rule Norway'.

In expectation of war, the Norwegian army mobilized and thousands of patriots flocked to the border. Equally cowed by Norway's strong navy, Stockholm backed down – on 7 June 1905, a national holiday in Norway (but not in Sweden!). Although the subsequent Treaty of Karlstad had Norway demolish all fortifications on its border with Sweden – a very unpopular clause – the treaty was implemented. Neighbourly relations were re-established that have held strong to this day.

Old King Oscar was less conciliatory. Piqued, he revoked the appointment of his second son, the 'Blue Prince' Carl, to the Norwegian throne.

Prime minister Michelsen applied on behalf of his kingless country to the 'Father-in-Law of Europe', Christian IX of Denmark, who accepted the nomination of his grandson, Carl.

Independent again, and for good. Prince Carl of Denmark's first action in his new realm was to ascertain his acceptability to his Norwegian subjects – by means of a referendum which, despite rumours of widespread republicanism, showed a solid majority in favour of a continued kingdom.

One cold November day in 1905, accompanied by his consort Maud and carrying on his arm their infant son, the new king walked proudly down the gangplank of the warship *Heimdal* to the cheers of his subjects crowding Oslo's Pier of Honour.

He took the name of Haakon VII, his son Alexander Carl that of Crown Prince Olav. Queen Maud was daughter of Britain's Edward VII (who is said to have been instrumental in Haakon's appointment – the magnificent British Embassy building in Oslo being Edward's reward). His Queen Alexandra was Danish, and Danish was the language spoken by the new royal family, something which Norwegians initially found alien. Like the English under Dutch-speaking William and the very German George II, however, they grew to accept the fact. And when the crown prince proved his prowess in that most Norwegian of sports, the ski-jump, and when even the frail little queen went skiing with her tall husband, all doubts were dispelled.

The king's sense of humour, like Prince Charles', relaxed official functions. 'Haakon belonged to no class, but to the people', as the poet Arnulf Øverland wrote during the War. The king himself reiterated that 'We are also king to the Communists'. Few critics could find partiality or flaws in Haakon's long eventful reign. The marriage of Crown Prince Olav in 1927 to his Swedish cousin, Princess Märtha, made a moment of patriotic jubilation amidst the economic gloom. In 1939 Olav and Märtha departed for what proved to be a triumphant tour of the USA. The success of this visit was of great significance: the lasting impression made by the royal couple, not only on Norwegian-Americans but even on the President, were to pay dividends in the difficult years of occupation and exile that lay ahead.

World War II. When war was declared in September 1939, the minority Labour government of Johan Nygaardsvold was in power. Foreign minister was the historian Halvdan Koht, who declared that 'the defence of the country depends on an alert and well-informed Foreign Service'.

In 1933 Norway had put into effect a new Defence Plan, which abolished the trusty old corps of permanent NCOs, and promoted senior sergeants and warrant officers to second and first lieutenant. The whole defence system had suffered: the Navy was rusting and obsolete; military and naval budgets were ridiculously low; the training period for conscripts was reduced to 48 days. Towards the end of the 1930s some politicians became aware of what was happening in the world around them, and a few aircraft were bought – including Italian Caproni bombers which were paid for with dried cod. At the start of 1940, Norway had on order 110 Curtis P-36 fighters, some Gloucester Gladiators and a few Douglas A-6 two-seater attack bombers. By April of that year some Curtis P-36s had arrived but were still in their crates.

Oslo, any 17th of May

In that same month of April 1940, Norway's 'alert Foreign Service' received the expected storm warnings. The Dutch military attaché in Berlin notified the Norwegian legation there of German troop movements, but no one took the warning seriously. Not even when, on 5 April, the German troopship *Rio de Janeiro* was sunk off the south Norwegian coast, and soldiers and horses were swimming in the sea, did Oslo react.

The attack on Norway was carried out, suddenly and rapidly, in what Germany called the *Weser-Übung* (Operation Weser). In the night of 8-9 April 1940, under the command of General Nikolaus von Falkenhorst, German naval units forced their way into Norway's major ports . . . without a single order to mobilize or resist being heard from the Labour government.

The king and his family, the government and parliament were saved by a lucky shot. Sailing up the Oslo Fjord, the *Blücher* was hit from the old guns at Oscarsborg: with her went down the German administration staff that, in the wake of the overnight putsch, was to move in and govern occupied Norway. Thanks to quick and resolute action on the part of the Speaker of Parliament, Carl Joachim Hambro, the whole assembly escaped safe to Hamar. There the Storting met and set to drafting the powers needed for the conduct of war. A German air raid interrupted the session and, on the afternoon of 9 April 1940, all moved twenty miles east to Elverum, where the draft of the government's 'Elverum Power of Attorney' was completed.

In an audience with King Haakon the following day the German minister, Dr Bräuer, demanded that a new Nazi government be formed and entrusted to Quisling. (The notorious Major Vidkun Quisling was leader of Norway's National Unity Party, which held only two per cent.) Having reported this to his cabinet, the king replied with a resounding *Nei!* He addressed the nation, calling on his countrymen to join forces in defending their independence and lawful government.

Orders were issued for mobilization, but only four days hence. Nevertheless, a number of units managed immediately to muster sufficient men to form companies and battalions (volunteers often skiing through the forests to join their officers or units). Resistance commenced, considerably impeding the German advance in many areas. The chief of Norway's general staff, Colonel Otto Ruge, was promoted general on 11 April and given command of the army. He led the defence with courage and tenacity until the bitter end.

The Allies mounted an intensive campaign to save Norway, but in vain. The Royal Navy was first on the scene: already on 9 April (after the loss of HMS *Glow-worm* the day before) HMS *Renown* had engaged the battle-ships *Gneisenau* and *Scharnhorst*, and the cruisers *Köln* and *Königsberg* had been sunk, the former in Christiansand, the latter in Bergen harbour.

Åndalsnes was the scene of the ill-fated landing of the British 148th Brigade on 18 April 1940. The Luftwaffe bombed out the Expeditionary Force and, after its evacuation, continued to bomb Åndalsnes into the ground. Beautifully rebuilt since, the town and neighbouring Veblungsnes are now home for some 3000 inhabitants – and a far greater annual number of visitors who fish for salmon and sea-trout in the teeming River Rauma, hike in the delightful Møre and Romsdal mountains or leap (with parachutes, but illegally) from the peaks of the nearby Trollveggen.

The town straddles the River Rauma, at its estuary with the spectacular Romsdalfjord. Railhead for the line from Oslo, it is linked by scenic roads through the Møre and Romsdal province to Ålesund, Molde and Christiansund and the breath-taking Trollstigveien.

Ten destroyers attacked the key northern port of Narvik the following day, and HMS *Warspite* the German fleet there on 13 April.

The British 148th Brigade landed at Åndalsnes on 18, the 15th Brigade on 23 April. In the north, a Scots Guards battalion disembarked on 14 April at Sjøvegan and the next day the 24th Brigade at Harstad, both in Troms province. They were followed on 29 April by the South Wales Borderers (at Håkvik) and on 6 May by the French Foreign Legion. Compatriots of the last, a battalion of Chasseurs Alpins had landed at Narvik on 28 April. The RAF was represented by a Gloucester Gladiator fighter squadron which established its base on Lesjaskogsvann in Gudbrandsdal on 25 April.

Two Polish battalions finally arrived to help the expeditionary force to the only victory of the Norwegian campaign (and the Allies' first success in World War II): at Narvik, after heavy fighting on 28 April, General Dietl's *Alpenjäger* (the Austrian Alpine Division) was driven back into Sweden. In overall command was Norway's chief of 6th Division, Major-General Carl G. Fleischer. The Norwegian Alta Battalion under Lieutenant-Colonel Arne D. Dahl performed conspicuously.

The Germans, concentrated in the south, pressed north, meeting fierce resistance around Namsos in north Trøndelag. Bodø, where the 3rd Independent Company had landed on 3 May, was largely obliterated by German bombs in the night of 27-28 May.

Norway was not so much defeated as sacrificed. As in 1814, her interests came second to those of, then the great powers', now the Allies' requirements elsewhere. The Wehrmacht was making such advances in France that Allied troops in Norway had to be withdrawn to reinforce the Western front. Left without support, the Norwegian 6th Division fought on until 7 June 1940 when, after 62 days of fighting, Norway capitulated. The army was demobilized, and General Ruge deported to a German PoW camp for the duration of the War. Determined to fight on, the king, crown prince and several officers and officials left Tromsø for London on board HMS *Devonshire* on 7 June. Several units of the Royal Norwegian Navy and some sea-planes also found their way to Britain.

In London, a substantial Norwegian administration was set up, centred on Kingston House in Hyde Park ('HQ Chairborne Division'). The Norwegian army established a training camp in Dumfriesshire and gradually a complete brigade was formed – as survivors arrived from torpedoed cargo ships or whalers, from the four corners of the globe (or over the North Sea from Norway). The navy was given ships by Britain and the USA and finally reached a strength of 52 units, plus training establishments in the UK and Canada. The Army Air Force and Fleet Air Arm, both under the arctic explorer and pilot, Rear-Admiral Hjalmar Riiser-Larsen, used the famous training camp 'Little Norway' in Toronto.

Norway's merchant navy – then the world's fourth largest in tonnage and first for modern tankers – responded to the king's appeal and served the Allied cause well. A central maritime command – Nortraship – was set up under the Oslo shipowner, Øivind Lorentzen. The entire Norwegian naval effort was financed by the income earned, and donated, by the fleet's 30,000 merchant seamen. Britain's minister of transport, Philip Noel-Baker, claimed that the Norwegian fleet's contribution to the Allied war effort was worth more than a million soldiers.

That fleet suffered heavy losses, especially when Admiral Dönitz's 'wolf packs', the deadly U-boats, set about the Atlantic convoys. Over half the fleet went down and 3670 sailors died.

'The Sinking of the *Scharnhorst* off North Cape'

Narvik miner

In Norway during the early War years, morale was at its lowest ebb. Those outside the country who knew anything about it – and a pitiful few they were – read reports to the effect that 'the Norwegians gave up and waved to the German troops marching in behind their bands'. Hambro, now Speaker, had served in 1938 as president of the League of Nations, and the international stature this gave him he now used to improve Norway's image in the free world. Crown Princess Märtha, who had escaped to Sweden with her three children, had sailed via Finland to the USA, where the bonds established in 1938, especially with President Roosevelt, served Norway well. Personal and public relations were also furthered by the work of such as Professor Jacob Worm-Müller and the Nobel Prize-winning novelist, Sigrid Undset. The American producer, Louis de Rochemont, directed one of Time Inc's monthly *March of Time* films entitled *Norway in Revolt.*

There the Resistance grew rapidly – in numbers and efficacity – but had initially to face formidable odds. Immediately after the occupation the Germans' attitude had been amicable towards their 'Aryan brothers'. 'Minister president' Quisling and his cronies set about building their *Nye Norge* ('New Norway') . . . with the help of several hundred thousand German rifles. Quisling in fact enjoyed considerable support in the early days. Many Norwegians volunteered for service on the Eastern front – first in Norwegian uniforms with Norwegian officers, later in SS-uniforms, as units of the Waffen-SS. In fairness, it should be remembered that not all of these were members of the Nazi Party: many believed that they were defending Norway against Bolshevism.

Their support was not rewarded. As opposition to the Germans grew, they removed their sheep's clothing and the Reichskommissar, Josef Terboven, unleashed on Norway the full force of Nazi rule. In Oslo the Gestapo installed itself in the government offices at Victoria Terrace. Concentration camps were built at Grini and Bredtvedt outside Oslo, at Falstad near Trondheim and at Sydspissen near Tromsø. (Of the 1409 Jews in Norway in 1940, 700 were deported to German concentration camps from which only fifteen returned.) Some 40,000 Norwegians were arrested, and thousands sent to Sachsenhausen, Buchenwald, Auschwitz, Belsen and Ravensbrück. In Norway, the Nazis executed 363 men and three women, while 38 men and one woman were tortured to death by Gestapo officers or their Norwegian agents, the *Stapo* ('State Police').

Rural resistance centred on the *'Gutta på skauen'*, 'the Boys in the Forest'. They were trained in great secrecy by Norwegian officers recruited in Britain; their numbers were swelled by, amongst other things, the closure of the university, and by 1945 totalled some 40,000.

One source of constant frustration to the Germans (and of elation to Norwegians, whose morale it lifted enormously) was the Linge Company. It was named after Reserve Captain (and peace-time actor) Martin Linge, who died leading the successful raid on Måløy at the mouth of the Sognefjord. Linge's men helped train the Boys in the Forest, sent important radio signals, assisted in the sinking of the *Bismarck* and *Tirpitz*, and sabotaged German installations and archives. The demolition of the German heavy-water plant at Rjukan was their work, and the sinking of a ferry-load of heavy water bound for Penemünde. In 1943 one Linge lieutenant, Gunnar Sønsteby (*alias 'Kjakan'*, the Jaw), saved thousands of young Norwegians from deportation to Germany's Russian front: they had been listed in a notorious register of 'Conscripted Labour Units' which the Nazis drew up and Sønsteby blew up.

Escaping the occupation forces was often as hazardous as resisting them. Thousands found their way out of occupied Norway, usually – like the Vikings – sailing small boats across to the Shetlands. Almost as many fled to Sweden and from transit camps there travelled on, sometimes via Russia, China or India, to join Norwegian forces in Britain or Canada. Flying low and by night, a clandestine airline (*Stockholmsruten*, the 'Stockholm route') brought Norwegian volunteers across to Leuchars in Scotland. Bernt Balchen from Christiansand carried 35 at a time in his B-24 Liberators on this brave run. In Sweden the Resistance mustered several companies of well-trained soldiers – known as *Reservepoliti* ('reserve police') to avoid arousing enemy suspicion.

As the War went on, Norwegian forces overseas grew impressively, under the political leadership of the defence minister in exile, Oscar Torp. The Navy was equipped with better ships – destroyers, corvettes, sub-marines and motor-torpedo boats – and played a sterling part in the sinking of the *Scharnhorst* and *Bismarck*. Under joint air command – of the Air Force and Fleet Air Arm – each of the five Norwegian squadrons worked in liaison with the RAF. Many Norwegian pilots served in British squadrons – fighters, night-fighters, bombers and liaison – and many ferried planes across the Atlantic. Naval squadrons 330(N) and 333(N) sank a number of U-boats as well as landing and picking up agents inside Norway. Fighter squadrons 331(N) and 332(N) performed magnificently at Dieppe; Norwegian commandoes took part in 1944 in the invasion of the Walcheren Islands.

On D-Day, eighteen Norwegian officers went ashore with the 52nd Lowland Division. Many died or were seriously wounded. Norwegian naval units took part in the landings, losing to German bombing the destroyer *Glaisdale*. Fighter squadrons 331(N) and 332(N) were also engaged, and the whole of 132(N) Wing took over forward airfields in France and served under the RAF until the armistice.

The closing days of the War cost Norway dear. As the victorious Russians forced the Nazis' Lapland Army back across north-eastern Norway, the German General Rendulic adopted scorched-earth tactics: the whole country east of Lyngen in Troms, most of the province of Finn-mark, was ravaged – houses burned, cattle slaughtered and the population sent south. The Russians came hard on the retreating Germans' heels; Norwegians led by Major-General Dahl and 'reserve police' units from Sweden shared the rigours of the advance across the plundered province.

The War ended with 350,000 German troops blocked in 'Fortress Norway'. Fortunately, they capitulated without resistance, General Thorne of the Allied Military Mission accepting the German surrender from General Böhme at Lillehammer on 8 May 1945.

Norway's government in exile entrusted the return to civilian rule to Paal Berg and the 'HL', the *Hjemmefrontens Ledelse* or Home-Front Leadership. Commander-in-chief since D-Day had been the then Crown Prince Olav, who landed at Oslo's Fornebu airfield on 13 May 1945. On 7 June King Haakon, Princess Märtha and the three royal children stepped from the barge of HMS *Devonshire* on to Oslo's Pier of Honour. The crowds were jubilant. On behalf of his people the king was officially welcomed by the mayor of Oslo (and later prime minister), Einar Gerhardsen, recently released from Sachsenhausen. Government powers were immediately invested in the pre-War Labour prime minister, Johan Nygaardsvold – the 44,000-odd, armed Home-Front Militia taking credit for the 'order, peace and discipline' that marked the transition.

Norway to Date. After the War the United States did not forget the Europe it had sacrificed so many lives to liberate. Named after the foreign secretary, General George C. Marshall, the Marshall Plan for the reconstruction of Europe provided material and interest-free loans to a total of fifteen billion dollars. Norway's share of this was $250 million – inestimable aid which by the 1950s had helped the country back on to its feet.

A common border with the USSR meant that Norwegians shared the West's apprehension of Stalin's actions in Eastern Europe and, when the North Atlantic Treaty Organization was set up on 4 April 1949, Norway was an early NATO-signatory. In the 1950s and 1960s the 'balance of terror' between NATO and the Warsaw Pact countries created an international climate in which Norwegian diplomats and statesmen proved their worth. Best known is Trygve Lie, the War-time foreign minister who became the UNs' first secretary-general.

Norway's governments, like Britain's, remained Labour for much of the immediate post-War period, the prime minister being repeatedly the former mayor of Oslo, Einar Gerhardsen. Interruptions came in 1963 when elections were won by John Lyng's non-Socialist coalition, and in 1965 when the Agrarian Party came to the fore in a new coalition government.

The Agrarian Party alone took a firm stand – negative – on the crucial question of Norway's membership of the EEC. Other parties like the Christian Democrats (and to a lesser extent the Conservatives) were and still are divided on this issue. In the early 1970s it was to make and break governments: it brought Labour to power in 1970 under Trygve Bratteli, who then resigned in 1972 when a referendum found against the Common Market. It had been preceded by a bitter campaign and was very closely run: 47% in favour and 53% against. The issue did not die with the referendum, and Norway's eventual membership of 'Europe' remains controversial.

The oil wealth of the 1970s went, say some, to politicians' heads, their handling of the economy was more *nouveau riche* than wise. Vast sums were allocated for development before a barrel of oil had been sold, and the spending spree indulged in by governments of the 1970s gave Norwegians a standard of living which revenue did not yet warrant. Theirs was far from a monetarist policy; inflation soared; Norwegians – and visitors – are still paying the penalty with some of Europe's highest prices.

Other repercussions aggravated the situation. The fisheries have suffered – though not directly because of oil – and this former source of Norway's wealth is jeopardized today. Inflated costs and wages have priced industry out of several export markets, and subsidies to the remaining farmers have put foodstuffs here amongst the world's most expensive. Most Norwegians agree that lower subsidies are needed but the farmers' lobby (*qua* the Agrarian Party) is strong. The public controversy over subsidies is naturally bound up closely with the long-term problem of Norway's joining the Common Market.

History will put back into perspective these issues of the day. Just as oil changed Norway's fortunes twenty years ago, other unforeseen factors may well bring new wealth – and new problems – a few years hence. One thing is certain: besides producing farmed fish now in hitherto undreamed-of quantities, Norway is attracting visitors more and more each year. From North America and western Europe in particular, tourism is booming, welcoming back the peoples of those lands the Vikings raided or discovered a thousand years ago.

Cities and Sites

Oslo is capital and, with 455,000 inhabitants, easily leads the list of Norway's cities. A municipal area of 175 square miles makes it, on paper, also one of the world's largest. Where both extent and population are concerned, it is however rather a late starter, having spent its first 800 years of fitful growth as an undistinguished provincial town still boasting in 1815 only 11,000 souls.

After his return from Byzantium and the timely death of his co-ruler, Magnus the Good, Harald Hardråde ('Hard-ruler'), the last of the Viking kings, in 1050 made his seat of government the fields and hills beneath the mountain of 'Eikaberg', where the River Alna meets the *Viken,* the Oslo Fjord. He called this capital Oslo, a name that survived until 1624 when in honour of the new king, Christian IV, it was replaced by Christiania. (This was in 1886 'Norwegianized' to Kristiania, 'Oslo' remaining in use throughout for the district known nowadays as Gamlebyen, the 'Old Town'.) In 1924 Norway celebrated the 300th anniversary of the name Christiania by dropping it: with effect from 1 January 1925 'Oslo' was again official.

Its origins and meaning are not for that any clearer. It is first recorded as *Ansloe, Opsloe* and *Aslo.* One theory is that Oslo is the *Os* (estuary) of the river Lo – a theory perturbed by the fact that Oslo's river has since earliest times been the Alna. The Field or Glade (*Lo*) of the god (*As*) is another solution proposed by the historian, Professor Edvard Bull, for the problem of Aslo/Oslo. Or perhaps Åslo, *Ås* being Norwegian for 'hill' and 'Hill Field' not unsuited to the site or inconceivable.

My favourite explanation came from a former Bulgarian ambassador to Norway. When I was welcoming his athletes, as chairman of the Athletic Association, I heard from him that schoolchildren in Sofia were taught that a Bulgarian princess had given Oslo its name. She, the story goes, had been captured by a Byzantine emperor, forcibly christened and carried off to Constantinople. There she fell in love with a captive Norse

Akershus, the name of the province adjacent to Oslo, is for visitors synonymous with the castle that, standing stark on the Aker promontory, dominates most vistas of the City Hall and centre. It was planned and built by Håkon V, to defend the city he had newly chosen as his capital in preference to Bergen. Begun in 1300, work was completed in 1308, just before the king's death.

No sooner was the fortress finished than it had to withstand attack by the Swedish Duke Eric – successfully, the site proving as impregnable then as in all offensives since. Håkon VI made of Akershus his royal residence, and at its gates in 1502 Knut Alvsson 'Three Roses' was murdered despite his flag of truce by the Dane, Henrik Krummedike. Struck by lightning in 1527, the fort was rebuilt in time to foil the attempts of Norway's last Catholic king, Christian II, to retake the kingdom with his Dutch mercenaries.

The present edifice, an impressive combination of strong fortress and elegant palace, is usually attributed to the famous Christian IV, 'Christian Quart' (1585-1648), whose masterbuilder, Hans van Steenwinckel, extended and embellished in the early 17th century.

There followed a long inconclusive siege by Charles XII of Sweden in 1712. Surviving every onslaught, the castle then succumbed to time: its state of disrepair by this century was such that Sinding Larsen's team, for all their skill, faced a formidable task of restoration. Work was later taken over by Arnstein Arneberg, architect of the City Hall, and after his death by the state. Akershus Castle is now the scene of banquets and other state functions. Thanks to the late Arno Berg, the 'Red Cross general' Hans C. Høegh, and the state antiquarian, Stephan Tschudi-Madsen, the public appreciates its splendours too.

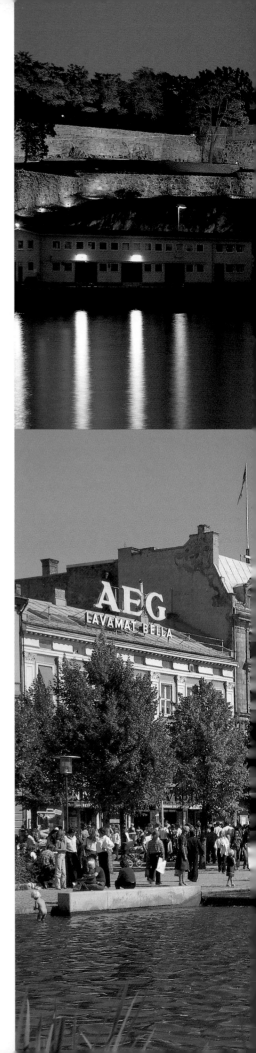

Akershus Castle on the Aker promontory (above)

Eidsvollplass, in Oslo's city centre

60

Oslo, Frognerkilen in the 1970s

prince, Araltes. When he with her help was released and returned to Norway, he showed his gratitude by giving the new capital her name: 'Oslava'. I was for a long time out on a limb with this theory until, addressing Rotarians on the subject, an Armenian member spoke up: he too had been taught the story at school in Istanbul.

The question of how the place should be pronounced is more social than academic: *Ossslo* with a hard *s*, as the well-to-do of Westend like to say, or the good colloquial *Oshlo* that we old hands prefer.

The 11th-century Oslo/Aslo/Åslo or Oslava was endowed by Harald Hardråde with a fine palace, churches and monasteries. His nobles were required to build their residences near by. For all that the result was no real metropolis. Fires and plagues impeded, respectively, urban expansion and population growth. The Black Death alone claimed some three quarters of the town's 3000 souls in 1349-50.

When the future capital was engulfed by fire on 24 September 1624, the Danish-Norwegian king, Christian IV, decided to move its site to the shelter of the guns of Akershus Castle, which had just been restored. The king, a distinguished architect and town-planner, himself designed his new city. Land was donated for richer citizens to build their homes in 'smarter' districts, in return for their financing craftsmen's quarters elsewhere. The new city, Christiania, was no sooner taking shape than the plague struck and carried off 1300 inhabitants. A generation later, it returned to claim another 1500 lives. The change of name did not save the city from frequent fires either – or from the Swedish Carl XII's siege of Akershus and destruction of many homes in 1716.

When the first census was taken in 1769, the population had risen to 7469. Most were almost certainly immigrants from other European countries. Craftsmen came to set up shop here; German and French officers were seconded to the Norwegian army; Dutch, German and Baltic businessmen controlled exports and shipping, smelting and ironworks. In 1785 Bishop Deichman established the library

Oslo Cathedral was inaugurated in 1697, a small cruciform building that replaced the old Trinity Church as the capital's principal place of worship. Named the Church of Our Saviour, the cathedral was (with the exception of the Akershus army chapel) Christiania's only church for over 150 years. Unlike many other Norwegian cathedrals, which predate the Reformation and are converted Catholic, the Oslo *Domkirke* ('cathedral church') is a purely Protestant creation. The exterior was reworked and the tower and spire added in 1849-50 by the architect Alexis de Chateauneuf. A century later, and thanks to the Oslo Savings Bank, the entire structure was restored and a new chapel consecrated. In charge was Arnstein Arneberg (of Akershus and City Hall fame); the heavy bronze doors were the work of Dagfinn Werenskiold (whose wood-carvings adorn the City Hall). Most impressive, the magnificent murals were painted by Hugo Louis Mohr. (Needing eggs to make tempera during War-time rationing, he was obliged to keep Black Market hens.)

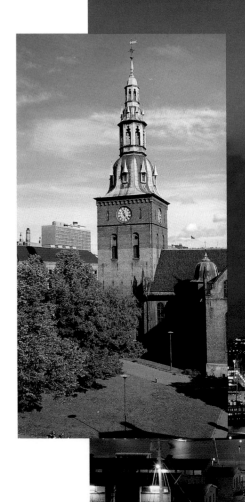

62

which is still the pride of Oslo, and in 1811 was built the Royal Frederick's University, the country's first.

Prior to 1814 Oslo was not so much a capital as residence of the viceroy or governor-general appointed by Copenhagen, and for the *Slottsloven*, an advisory council with limited powers. After Napoleon's defeat and the Treaty of Kiel, however, the town took on a new rôle as capital of a freer Norway (though bound in a joint monarchy and common Foreign Service to 'big brother' Sweden). Little by little those buildings appeared that characterize a national capital; the somnolent little 'provincial' town seemed to awake. The impressive Royal Palace was commenced in 1825, the State hospital constructed in 1826. The National Gallery of Art and the Christiania Theatre followed in 1837. In 1854 the rail-link with Eidsvoll necessitated the new Oslo railway station, and in 1866 Norway's 150 MPs moved into

Karl Johans gate, Oslo's main street (above)

City Hall and Aker Brygge (left)

their new Storting on the hill south of the main street later called Karl Johans gate. With traffic increasing, the first lines were in 1875 laid for trams, horse-drawn of course. The cramped city expanded – from 3½ to six square miles – thanks to boundaries redrawn in 1878.

The Industrial Revolution affected Christiania as it did other major European cities: the Akers-elv became an important source of energy. Every waterfall along this short but vigorous river powered textile- and flour-mills, workshops and smelting plants. The work-force these needed came not only from the nearby city but from the most remote valleys: the drift to the towns competed with the lure of the

New World in this period of mass emigration. In the textile industry in particular, hundreds of women were employed – small children too.

On 15 January 1891 was born Oslo's most distinguished son and 'eternal mayor', Rolf Stranger – a historic link with Norway's past until his death in 1990. As a teenager Stranger was there when the late King Olav was carried ashore at Oslo's Pier of Honour on the arm of his father, the new King Haakon VII. Stranger was still a law student when, in 1914, Christiania and Norway celebrated the 100th anniversary of independence (with a great exhibition which elderly people today claim 'put Norway on the map').

During and for some time after the First World War, things went well, largely due to Norway's neutrality and profitable shipping (which had nevertheless sustained heavy losses of material and Norwegian seamen's lives). There followed the Depression years of hunger and poverty. Norway's famous post-War prime minister, Einar Gerhardsen, called these 'the hard Thirties' – and hard they certainly were. In spite of this a far-sighted mayor, Hieronymus Heyerdahl, succeeded in financing and began to build the splendid City Hall. Interrupting the project was a minor inconvenience of the Nazi occupation during World War II.

The post-War reconstruction and modernization of Oslo was largely the work of Brynjulf Bull and the indefatigable Stranger. In 1947 the capital was merged administratively with the neighbouring province of Aker, and the forests to the north, south and east included in the municipal area. Oslo's electoral system was changed in 1986 so that a *Byrådet,* or 'city government', is appointed by whichever party has a majority of the city council's 85 seats. The chairman of the Byrådet is the city's political leader, and he and his 'cabinet' are paid a salary.

Many outstanding citizens have served as mayor since the Municipal Laws were passed in 1837. Some (like Fredrik Stang, Oscar Torp and Einar Gerhardsen) later became prime ministers, others (like Stranger) MPs, but most devoted their time and attention exclusively to their native city. Mayor for many years (until 1990) was Albert Nordengen, whose smile became something of a hall-mark for Oslo, the 'Big-hearted City'. The slogan is not to everyone's liking as poverty and suffering can still be found behind the sunny façade. (The suffering, Norwegians say, seems to be greatest amongst the 60,000 municipal employees – to judge by the statistics for their days off and sick leave. These average 30 per employee per year – a national record – and why so many are needed and these so often sick, nobody knows.)

In recent years Oslo has been marred by seemingly endless building sites and excavations, but the butterfly is slowly emerging from the chrysalis of construction work. Dilapidated buildings are reappearing from behind hoardings as monumental office blocks, shopping malls and modern hotels. The former shipyards and disused docks have been converted into 'highly desirable' (and pricey) condominiums and shopping precincts such as the much-publicized Aker Brygge complex. On 24 February 1989 Mayor Nordengen drove down the new tunnel beneath the city centre to ignite the final charge. This long, deep and costly project will enable traffic to flow fast under Oslo, beneath Akershus Castle and old Christiania. The present Rådhusgate, now congested and dangerous, will become a pedestrian precinct. Residents and foreigners are finding once again that the capital is an attractive and motivating place to live in or visit.

Oslo boasts 50 museums, over 30 cinemas, and theatres ranging from the venerable Nationaltheatret with its Henrik Ibsen repertoire to the brand-new Norske Teatret. The first director of the impressive National Opera was Kirsten Flagstad, star of the Metropolitan Opera. Based on a fine new concert hall, the Oslo Philharmonic enjoys world-wide renown.

The City Hall (*Rådhuset*) is Oslo's focal centre. Opposite the Pier of Honour (so often a literal landmark in Norway's history), its site of Piperviken had been a relative slum until work began in 1931 on the project first envisaged in 1915 by the Conservative mayor, Hieronymus Heyerdahl. He launched the building fund with a personal donation of one million kroner, most of the balance being raised by expropriation and sale of the land around. Of the several plans tendered, that of Magnus Poulson and Arnstein Arneberg won first prize. After years of clearance (both administrative and physical – of the site itself) the foundation-stone was laid in 1931. The War intervened and it was only in 1950 (the 900th anniversary of Harald Hardråde's founding of Oslo) that the completed project was ready for inauguration by King Haakon VII.

Most think of the City Hall as a monumental red-brick pile, but it is in fact built of concrete, the 1½ million hand-made bricks being a four-sided façade. The structure covers 48,230 square feet and the striking décor inside and out – of sculptures, wood-carving and painting by various artists – has Norway's history and the occupation as leitmotivs.

The Royal Palace (*Slottet*) is King Harald's official residence and home. When he is in residence, his red and gold standard flutters from the roof. A split in the flag denotes that Crown Prince Haakon is acting head of state in his father's absence. The palace commands from its eminence the main street now called Karl Johans gate. The 55 acres of woodland and park that surround it are a public thoroughfare into town. Yet this hilly site near the Uranienborg Forest was at the time of building on the outskirts of the capital. Its conception was Bernadotte's, after his accession as King Carl XIV. A Danish officer and lawyer, H. D. F. Linstow, was commissioned as architect in 1823 and the foundation-stone laid in 1825. Because however of repeatedly changed plans, the palace was not completed until 1848, in time for the new king, Oscar I, and his French queen, Josephine.

Fountains and the façade of Oslo's City Hall

The Royal Palace, Oslo

Spring Day on Karl Johan (1890)

The Day After (1894-95)

Edvard Munch, in a country where busts and statues honour worthies on most street corners, is not commemorated with a single effigy. Yet for the art world of the west, Munch is Norway's best-known painter.

That Munch's art lacks glee is usually attributed to childhood loss. Born in Løten on 12 December 1863, the artist was five when his mother died. The depressive tendencies inherited from his doctor father, Christian, worsened with the slow death of a favourite sister, Sophie, when Munch was aged fourteen. The engineering studies he began in 1879 were abandoned one year later in favour of painting, early subjects being self-portraits and the controversial *The Sick Child*.

Studying art, and sharing an Oslo studio with six fellow students, Munch was soon a full-fledged member of the 'Norwegian Bohemia'. Christian Krohg

was doyen of that studio, and much of Munch's first work appears modelled on his. Studies in Paris, at the Salon and the Louvre, widened Munch's horizons after 1885. Working alternately in Oslo and France (Paris, Saint-Cloud, Le Havre and Nice), Munch from now on exhibited regularly, and with some success (except in Berlin, in 1892, where press and public protests closed his show within a week). German contacts (with the 'Black Piglet Circle') account for increasing visits to Berlin, where in 1894 his first etchings were completed. Though appealing perhaps to a smaller public, Munch's 17,000 prints, lithographs, etchings, drawings, woodcuts and aquarelles are seen by certain specialists as his finest work.

By 1900, no longer 'Bohemian', Edvard Munch is almost establishment. A study of his work appears in German; a German, Gustav Schiefler,

begins cataloguing his graphic works; the Cassirer Gallery in Berlin acquires the rights to all his engravings, Commeter in Hamburg to all the paintings. The Weimar Art Academy puts a studio at the painter's disposition in 1904; friezes are commissioned, and in 1906 stage-sets for *Hedda Gabler* and *Ghosts*.

Already in 1900, however, Munch had made a first visit to a Swiss sanatorium. Increasingly neurotic, and alcoholic, he suffered a nervous breakdown in 1908. He recovered sufficiently to return in 1909 and commence work on the murals of the Oslo University *Aula*, the Great Hall that houses the Nobel Peace Prize ceremony. They were completed, amidst controversy, in 1914.

Travels and exhibitions, new and retrospective, occupied Munch between the Wars; but an eye ailment

handicapped him and in 1936 brought
work to a halt on the Oslo City Hall
murals begun in 1928. In 1937, 82 of his
paintings in German galleries received
the accolade of being condemned as
'degenerate'; the artist refused all
contact with the Nazis during the
occupation, and enjoyed in 1942 a
first exhibition in the USA. On 23
January 1944 he died peacefully at
the Ekely home he had bought,
near Oslo, in 1926.

Norwegians are proud of the Gustav
Vigeland Sculpture Park and Museum
in Oslo's Frogner Park; the City Fathers
in 1924 proudly endowed the 55-year-
old artist with these 80 acres; the pride
and self-assurance of his performance
is unwaveringly stated in the 192
groups of 650 figures here.

Adolf Gustav Vigeland was born
some five years after Munch – on 11
April 1869. He was almost literally a
born sculptor: his father was a cabinet-
maker, in the south-coast town of
Mandal, and design and carving were
no doubt learned at his knee. At the age
of twenty, trained by the sculptor Brynjulf Bergslien, Vigeland entered a first
group at the 1889 Autumn Exhibition.

Scholarships permitted visits first to
Copenhagen, where he studied under
Thorvaldsen and Vilhelm Bissen, then
to Paris, Berlin, Florence, Rome and
England. A first municipal commission, for the Frogner fountain in 1907,
formed the nucleus of his subsequent
life's work. In 1915 his grandiose
scheme was submitted: for a monumental (one-man) sculpture park
to be planned around the fountain.
This, with the massive Monolith under
way, the City Fathers approved in
1924. (Quarried on the Iddefjord near
Halden, the 55-foot block had been
brought by barge to Oslo and man-
handled into place in the park,
where Vigeland, working inside
an ad hoc tower, adorned it with
its 121 *ujamaa* figures.)

In return for consecrating his next
twenty years to the project, Vigeland
requested and was granted a studio
and home near by. This, the present
Vigeland Museum, is where he lived
and worked until his death on 12
March 1943. He had by then further
contributed the main gates, 58 pieces of
sculpture for the bridge, the 'labyrinth'
and a children's ferry for the lake (plus
many statues that a levy on Oslo's
cinemas may yet enable the
authorities to place).

The Kon-Tiki Museum was

built to house the balsa-wood raft on which Thor Heyerdahl, in 1947, drifted some 5000 miles to prove his supposition that the Polynesians originated in South America – and to win himself singular fame as this century's most outstanding nautical explorer.

Born at the beginning of World War I – at Larvik on 6 October 1914 – Heyerdahl saw his first travels cut short by World War II: from research amongst the coastal Indians of British Columbia, he returned to serve with the Royal Norwegian Air Force. In 1941 he first made known his theory that Polynesia may have been populated from South America. By 1947 he had the finance and the information required to build *Kon-Tiki* – from materials available in antiquity – and on 28 April, with three Norwegians and one Swede, he set sail from Callao in Peru. Winds and currents alone propelled the flimsy vessel to Raroia, in the Tuamotu group of islands, where landfall was made on 7 August. With his subsequent book translated into 60 languages and his film of the voyage awarded a 1952 Oscar, Heyerdahl could consider his theory vindicated.

A second theory – that the ancient Egyptians could have reached the Americas in papyrus boats – was launched inauspiciously in 1969: *Ra I* sank. But, built to designs depicted inside the pyramids, *Ra II* in 1970 successfully crossed the Atlantic. Leaving Safi in Morocco on 17 May, Heyerdahl arrived in Barbados on 12 July. His six-man crew was chosen from different nationalities (and very differing mentalities): this brave voyage of historical exploration explored human relationships too.

The *Ra* sailed under the auspices and flag of the United Nations, and Heyerdahl's interests have mainly centred since on problems of international co-operation and ecology. Awarded honours, medals and distinctions by heads of state and scientific bodies, and honorary doctorates by several universities, Thor Heyerdahl remains a friendly, soft-spoken 'citizen of the world'. When in Europe, he lives in a small Italian village; his monument was recently unveiled in his home town of Larvik; his latest work, again in South America, is on a possible Phoenician and ancient Egyptian presence there.

The *Fram*, in modern eyes, is

an unspectacular craft: 128-foot, displacement 800 tons, technically a three-masted barquentine or 'topsail schooner', and with only her unusual hull design of any apparent interest. Yet the *Fram* made possible the two greatest feats of polar exploration: Nansen's crossing of the Arctic Ocean and Amundsen's triumph (over Scott) at the South Pole. No other ship has ever sailed so far north or south.

The Norwegian Fridtjof Nansen was already a veteran authority on the polar regions when in 1890 he published his theory that currents crossed the Arctic Ocean: that an ice-bound vessel would not remain immobile but be carried by them on a predictable course. The problem was to construct a vessel that the pack-ice would not crush. A grant from the Norwegian Storting and enthusiastic private investment enabled Nansen and Otto Sverdrup to design the boat that Colin Archer built. The risk of destruction by ice was overcome by means of a triple hull – the two innermost of oak – so shaped that under the pack-ice's pressure the vessel would be forced upward and free.

Commissioned on 3 June 1893, the *Fram* set sail three weeks later, captained by Sverdrup and with Nansen in charge of research. They left the last Norwegian port, Vardø, on 21 July and were by 22 September locked in the arctic ice. There they sat for eighteen months, the *Fram* surviving the pack-ice and drifting satisfactorily in accordance with the currents Nansen predicted. Disappointed, however, that these were not bringing them closer to the pole, Nansen set off on foot on 14 March 1895, with Hjalmar Johansen and three dog-sleds. By 7 April their attempt had been frustrated by the ice's constant breaking and shifting.

The rest is epic, and fortuitous: Nansen and Johansen trekked to Franz Josef's Land, huddled there in a simple hut through the winter of 1895-96, then lashed together two kayaks and paddled them across the Arctic Ocean to Cape Flora. Where, amidst the polar desolation, they arrived to find the English explorer, Frederick Jackson. Aboard his *Windward* they reached Vardø on 13 August 1896 – the same day that the *Fram*, ice-bound for three long years, broke free off Spitsbergen.

Laid up, and designed to become a museum, the *Fram* was saved by 'polar competition'. Roald Amundsen, emulating Nansen, thought to drift closer to the North Pole by approaching via the Bering Strait; but on 6 April 1909 came news of the American Robert E. Peary's claim to have reached the pole first. As the Siberian route would entail a voyage round Cape Horn, Amundsen set his sights, secretly, on the South Pole instead. Sailing from Christiansand on 10 August 1910, he worked furtively and single-handed on the detailed planning of the triumph to come.

The English explorer he was to worst, Robert Falcon Scott, had set sail for the South Pole on 15 June 1910; in Melbourne, on 12 October, he received a telegram from Madeira: 'Am going south – Amundsen'. In Funchal the Norwegian also disclosed his South Pole plans to an enthusiastic crew. They sailed the *Fram* to the Ross Sea and, in the Bay of Whales on 14 January 1911, split into three groups: three men disembarked to reconnoitre Edward VII Land; the *Fram* under Captain Thorvald Nilsen departed to explore the Antarctic Ocean (sailing further south – 71° 41' – than any previous vessel), while Amundsen with five companions set off for the South Pole.

They reached it on 14 December 1911, raised the Norwegian flag and returned safely to the Bay of Whales, where the *Fram* re-embarked them and, four days later on 31 January 1912, sailed clear of the Antarctic ice. On 18 January Captain Scott and his five men had arrived at the South Pole to find the Norwegian flag flying. They perished on the trek back, within a few miles of the 'One-ton Camp' that would have saved them.

On 16 July 1914 the *Fram* came home to Norway, and there lay neglected for the next fifteen years. Widespread sympathy for the need to preserve her was frustrated by cost (and repeated committees) until in 1929 Lars Christensen had her towed to the Framnes shipyard in Sandefjord for the restoration that Otto Sverdrup supervized until his death in 1930. The work was completed by May 1935, when the *Fram* was towed to Bygdøy and hauled ashore to her last resting place.

The Viking Ship Museum

was designed by Arnstein Arneberg in 1913 and houses the two finest surviving Viking vessels – the 9th-century Gokstad and Oseberg ships – plus the remnants and contents of two lesser burials.

The 76' 5" Gokstad Ship was excavated on the same-named farm at Sandefjord in 1880, the 70' 11" Oseberg Ship on the farm of that name in Sem, Vestfold, in 1904. Also on display are the fragment-ary Tune Ship found at Rolvsøy, Østfold, in 1867 and the very vestigial Borre Ship discovered in 1850-52.

All were used for Viking burials: surmounted by a funerary chamber (from which three of the incumbents' skeletons and sundry grave goods have been recovered), they were covered by a burial mound, the clay of which preserved the wood, metalware, leather and textiles interred.

Viking ships, like those of ancient Rome, are usually classified by their number of oars, their 'oaring' (-*æring*) e.g. *sexæring* for a six-oared vessel or *færing* for the four-oared boat such as was found inside the Gokstad Ship. When larger size required that each rower man a single oar, terminology turned to the number of 'thwarts' or rowing benches. The Gokstad and Oseberg ships are samples of the 15 and 16-*sesse*, 'bencher'. With two rowers per bench, plus look-out, captain etc., their complement would have been about 35 men.

Oak was the wood preferred by the *skipasmed* ('ship's smith') but ash, beech, alder, birch, lime and willow were also used. An exception was the mast, made usually of fir, and stayed with ropes of walrus hide. A rudimentary rudder was fixed not astern but to the starboard (i.e. 'steer-board'). The 'nautical gargoyles' that account for the popular name 'dragon ships' were detachable, and apparently always removed before a longship returned to its home port, for fear of scaring off friendly spirits. Specialists call them 'animal head posts' and state that their function is not known: the effect on an enemy who sighted on the horizon the dragon heads of a full Viking *leidang*, a fleet of 720 ships, is easily surmised.

The Oseberg Ship in the Viking Ship Museum

The Holmenkollen ski-jump dominates the Oslo skyline from afar, a literal and figurative landmark in this most Norwegian of sports. From a long tradition of cross-country (but not downhill or 'Alpine') skiing, competition jumping developed relatively recently, with the first events at Huseby, Oslo, in 1879 and at Holmenkollen in 1892. The small ski-jump erected for the latter allowed of a record of 70' 6".

Reconstructed for the 1952 Winter Olympics, the jump was again rebuilt in 1981 for the 1982 World Championships – and the record soared to 359 feet. Besides the ski-jump's panoramic 195-foot summit, Holmenkollen also offers the Ski Museum of ancient and modern equipment, including that used by Amundsen and Nansen, and downhill the Besserud Lake.

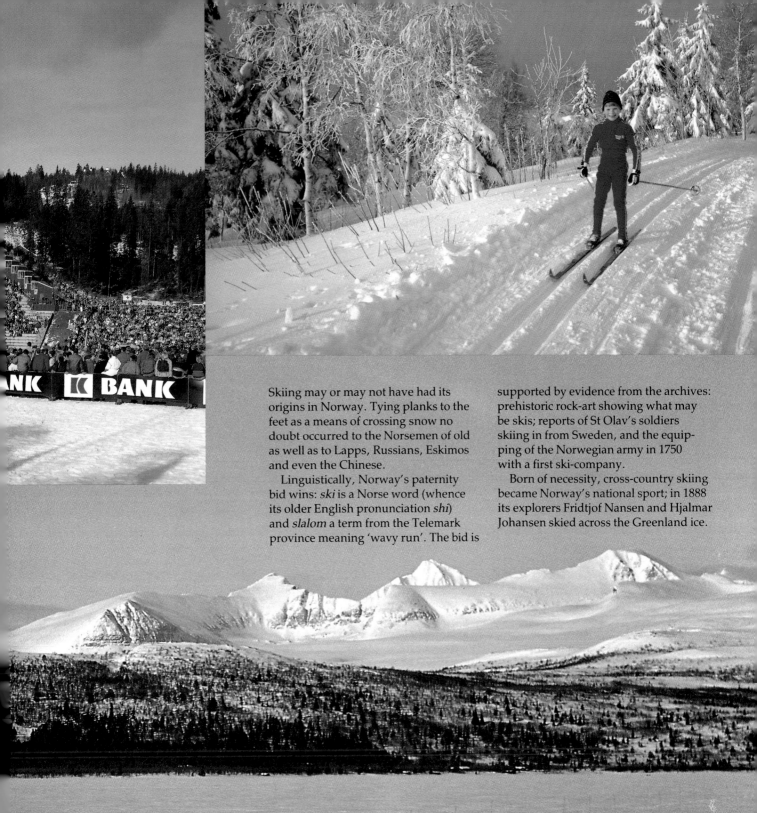

Skiing may or may not have had its origins in Norway. Tying planks to the feet as a means of crossing snow no doubt occurred to the Norsemen of old as well as to Lapps, Russians, Eskimos and even the Chinese.

Linguistically, Norway's paternity bid wins: *ski* is a Norse word (whence its older English pronunciation *shi*) and *slalom* a term from the Telemark province meaning 'wavy run'. The bid is supported by evidence from the archives: prehistoric rock-art showing what may be skis; reports of St Olav's soldiers skiing in from Sweden, and the equipping of the Norwegian army in 1750 with a first ski-company.

Born of necessity, cross-country skiing became Norway's national sport; in 1888 its explorers Fridtjof Nansen and Hjalmar Johansen skied across the Greenland ice.

Downhill runs however remained a precarious problem, depending on the skier's sense of balance (and one long wooden pole). The innovations of Sondre Norheim, a native of Telemark, revolutionized the sport. Giving the ski its modern 'waisted' shape and a heel-strap of rope, he introduced the Telemark and Christiania turns as a means of controlling downhill runs. His bindings, though, had no lateral support and still in the 1890s a first skiing manual advised: 'On the descent, the ski-runner leans back on his stick and shuts his eyes. Then he darts downward . . . and continues until he can no longer breathe. He then throws himself sideways on the snow'.

The experiments of an Austrian, Matthias Zdarsky, resulted in the modern metal toe-piece (which prevents the foot slipping sideways) and in the all-important stem turn. Thanks to the handbook he published in 1896 (and to English enthusiasts such as the well-known Methodist minister, Henry Lunn), the centre of interest in downhill skiing shifted south to the Alps. Norway remained the bastion of the combined cross-country and ski-jump, which Norwegians consider naturally the more demanding sport. They prove their point by holding more Olympic medals and world records in this discipline than any other nation.

Bergen. Like Rome or Lisbon, Norwegians often say, their second city, Bergen, spreads over seven hills. Unlike the southern counterparts, however, Bergen and its backdrop of hills face the North Sea and its rain-laden winds. Local girls may be pretty in traditional costume, but the umbrella has become the city's unofficial emblem, the raincoat is normal 'native dress'.

That Bergen over the centuries turned more towards Britain and northern Germany than the rest of Norway may perhaps be due to a like climate; a more probable cause is the natural barrier at its back. Communications with Oslo were easier by sea until the completion in 1909 of that feat of engineering, the Oslo-Bergen railway (*Bergensbanen*).

Historical detachment has made for modern singularities. The 211,200 residents of this 'western capital' are considered by their compatriots, and consider themselves, as something of a class apart, rather like Texans in American terms. Their pride in their city is intense – and very vocal. Every Bergenser knows his city's anthem. The National Day parade held throughout Norway each 17 May is in Bergen designated differently: 'the Procession'.

Its face to the sea, its harbour safe and large, Bergen turned naturally to maritime trade. Besides Britain, northern Germany was an early commercial partner, and links with the latter became so close that by 1343 Bergen was considered a member of the Hanseatic League (the mercantile and political union of Baltic city-states – to which England's Cinque Ports do not bear comparing).

For centuries Bergen flourished while Oslo floundered. The capital's only riposte is that Bergen is twenty years its junior, being founded in 1070 by Olav III Kyrre (born, of course, in Oslo). Vying with Trondheim as capital of the much-disputed kingdom, Bergen blossomed 200 years later when King Håkon IV developed there a residence worthy of his aspirations. Bjørgvin (as it was then known) was embellished with not only churches and, in 1261, the noted Håkonshallen. From the flourishing port set forth the ambassadors sent to Håkon's fellow sovereigns far and wide. With them went the hawks to be presented, that the royal falconry in Bergen had trained.

One long-term activity resulted in disaster. In 1349 a merchant vessel arrived from England carrying not only trade goods but also Black rats and the Black Death. The newly created Hanseatic town was ravaged by plague for two years. Fires followed and, despite the rain, remained a hazard: 2500 homes were in 1528 gutted by what Norwegians call the 'red rooster'.

The end of the '400-year-long night' gave Bergen, like Oslo, a new sense of direction and prosperity. The museum established in 1825 was later to become the University of Bergen. The fine theatre, *Den Nationale Scene*, followed in 1850, and six years later Bergensers witnessed the birth of their first *Buekorps*. The 'Bow-and-arrow Companies' proliferated, becoming an institution which still influences local attitudes. The first sign of spring is heralded in this western capital by the sound of the drumming and quick march of the

The *Statsraad Lehmkuhl*, a 1701-ton, steel three-masted barque, lies magnificent at anchor in Bergen harbour, the city's floating hall-mark. German-built in 1914, she was launched as *Grossherzog Friedrich August*; like her sister-ships, the *Grossherzogin Elisabeth* and *Prinzessin Eitel Friedrich,* she was designed as a training ship for the German merchant navy, with a complement of 240 cadets. Having served Germany in the Great War, the vessel formed part of post-War reparations. A Bergen businessman (and later minister of labour), Kristofer D. Lehmkuhl, acquired her when the city's old corvette *Alfen* proved no longer fit for naval training. She was renamed in Lehmkuhl's honour (the *Statsraad* meaning Cabinet Minister). With a complement of 170 boys and crewmen she has carried off prizes in several Tall Ship races and, despite recurrent financial problems, represents Bergen worthily on naval occasions overseas.

Bergen's famous flower market

The *Statsraad Lehmkuhl* (right)

uniformed boys armed with their wooden rifles.

A much-needed fire brigade was introduced in 1863 and electricity in 1900. Other Norwegians, themselves rarely reticent, joke about the loquacity of Bergen folk – a joke given new dimensions when in 1882 the telephone let Bergen talk with the outside world. By incorporating nearby districts, Bergen's urban area steadily grew: Kalfaret, Møhlenpris, Nygård and Sandviken in 1876, Årstad in 1915, Gyldenpris in 1921 and the Fylling valley in 1955. Finally in 1972, the city engulfed the neighbouring municipalities of Arna, Åsane, Fana and Laksevåg, but lost its status as a separate province.

In recognition of its people's drive and acumen, the College of Business Administration Studies was sited in Bergen in 1936, as was a university in 1948 and subsequently the Directorate of Fisheries with its famed Oceanographic Research Institute and the aquarium at Nordnes, Europe's largest.

With Edvard Grieg as its most distinguished son, Bergen naturally boasts a Grieghallen, a modern concert hall that since 1953 accommodates the annual International Festival of music, drama and ballet. The Grand Prix of the Eurovision Song Contest was recently staged here and the resident music society, Harmonien, is well known.

Edvard Grieg, Ludvig Holberg, Ole Bull, Harald Sæverud, Christian Michelsen, Agnes Mowinckel, Carl Joachim Hambro and Sissel Kyrkjebø . . . Bergen's roll of honour in arts, literature and politics compensates for its performance in sport, a national preoccupation. The rain, and relatively snow-free winters, are the usual pretext except where football is concerned. There no Bergenser would ever admit that Brann is anything less than Norway's best (whatever the team's position in the league tables may be).

Troldhaugen ('Troll Hill') is the wooden hilltop home that Edvard Grieg bought after the success of his best-known works, *Peer Gynt* and the Concerto in A minor. He lived and worked here till his death on 4 September 1907, he and his wife Nina being buried near by in a simple cliff-tomb.

Norway's most famous composer was born in Bergen on 15 June 1843, to a family of merchants, immigrants from Aberdeenshire in the 1700s. His musical education was begun by his mother and completed at the Leipzig Conservatoire. Graduating in Sweden in 1861, he made his musical début in Bergen in 1862 before moving to Copenhagen in 1863. There he studied under Gade, befriended Rikard Nordraak (composer of Norway's national anthem '*Ja, vi elsker*') and, grief-stricken when the latter died in 1866, wrote his Funeral March.

Love for his cousin, the opera-singer Nina Hagerup, prompted the song '*Jeg elsker Deg*', 'I love you'. Marrying Nina, Grieg moved to the capital in 1868, as conductor of the philharmonic orchestra. From 1869 to '77 the Griegs lived in Rome, friends of Franz Liszt. Honoured by his fatherland, Grieg returned in 1877, to set up home in Hardanger. His concert tours overseas were frequent, and public acclaim overwhelming. Like Liszt (but unlike

the hapless Munch), the composer enjoyed living fame.

Staying close to his musical roots, Grieg drew on old Norwegian folksongs and traditional instruments like the eight-stringed fiddle. It was at Henrik Ibsen's request, and as music for his stage-play, that *Peer Gynt* was written. For Bjørnstjerne Bjørnson, Grieg composed the libretto of the opera *Sigurd Jorsalfar* and the songs *Bergljot, Landkjenning* and *Olav Tryggvason*.

Bergen, statue of the composer Edvard Grieg (above left) and Troldhaugen, his final home, now a museum (above)

Trondheim, an early capital, is now the third Norwegian city with 136,700 inhabitants. (In the late 1940s its population took it to second place above its southern rival, Bergen, but sterling work by the Bergensers – less effective on the football field than in bed – had by the 1950s restored their position.)

If not perhaps 'the world's most ideal town', as the official blurb has it, Trondheim enjoys a delightful site where the River Nid meets the Trondheim Fjord. The compact and attractive city centre is nicely balanced between commercial, academic and historic, with its industry parked sensibly amidst suburban green.

The name is a contentious compromise. The first settlement was founded by Olav Tryggvason as *Kaupangen i Trondheimen*, the 'trading town in the province of Trondheim'. It was later baptized Nidaros, a name retained in the fine cathedral (and clearly derived from its River Nid). For centuries the resident Trønders had called their home *Tronhjæm*. When in 1929 the Storting, for historical reasons, proposed to revive 'Nidaros', local protest was such that 'Trondheim' was adopted as official compromise. The Trønders ignore that, saying *Tronhjæm* as before.

The city entered history as residence of the Ladejarls, the wealthy earls of Lade. From this rich region, the Trøndelag, the Ladejarl Håkon Sigurdsson ruled Norway until 995, when he died fleeing from his successor, Olav Tryggvason. Though born in eastern Norway, the latter (as Olav I) founded Kaupangen i Trondheimen two years later.

The settlement's rise to fame and prosperity it owes to Olav II. Norway's later patron, St Olav, he was killed at the battle of Stiklestad in 1030 and interred in the Church of St Clement he had built in 1016. The disinterment in 1031 of his body, unblemished, and the spring that promptly appeared on the spot ensured his canonization – and the establishment of Nidaros as a mediaeval place of pilgrimage. The pious throng was densest on the *Olsok* days, around the anniversary of Olav's death on 29 July. In 1897, for its 900th anniversary, Trondheim revived the Olsok, and now celebrates it annually as a ten-day festival.

Trondheim, the Nidaros Cathedral (left); its rose window, the work of Gabriel Kielland from 1907 to 1934 (below), and the central Munkegata, 'Monk Street' (right)

Stiftsgården, on the main Munkegata (Monk Street), is Scandinavia's largest wooden building, with 70 rooms and an area of 12,380 square feet. Built in 1774-78 as the private home of the widowed Cecilia de Schøller, it was acquired by the state in 1800, to house the provincial governor, and in 1906 became Trondheim's royal residence.

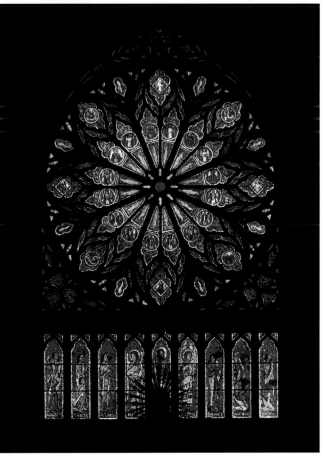

Olav's son, Magnus the Good, extended the city, and vestiges of his contribution have been excavated in Søndre gate, 'South Street'. In 1152 Cardinal Brakespeare visited Nidaros and there installed an archbishop, and in 1179, at nearby Kalvskinnet (the Calf Hide), 'king' Sverre and his Birkebeiners defeated Erling Skakke and annihilated most of Norway's nobles. The low-born Birkebeiners, most from the surrounding region of Trøndelag, controlled the kingdom until 1217. In that year legitimacy was restored in the person of Håkon IV, who had his regent and rival, Skule, killed in the Trondheim monastery of Elgeseter.

As 'primate' of Norway, the last archbishop of Nidaros, Olav Engelbrektsson, fiercely resisted the Lutheran advance but was in 1537 forced out of office and into exile, to be replaced by a Protestant 'superintendent'. Trondheim was captured and occupied by the Swedes in 1564, and the whole region ceded (temporarily) to Sweden by treaty in 1658. Peter Jansen Wessel was born here in 1690 – to become before the age of 30 the Vice-admiral Tordenskjold who defeated the fleet of Carl XII of Sweden at Dynekilen in 1716. Two years later the latter besieged Nidaros . . . in the only military action ever to have damaged it. Fires, though, were frequent and the greatest, in 1681, led to the rebuilding of the present city centre by the Luxembourger general, Caspar de Cicignon.

Besides being the scene of many coronations, from Karl Knutsson Bonde to Haakon VII (the late king having been merely blessed here in 1958), Trondheim is the birthplace of many distinguished Norwegians: the post-War prime minister, John Lyng, and the present president of the Storting, Jo Benkow. The long-serving prime minister, Johan Nygaardsvold, had his origins near by at Hommelvik. In sport the city excels: Norway's best footballers are probably the Trondheim team Rosenborg. The handball clubs Freidig and Sverresborg provided most of Norway's Olympic bronze team; in speedskating Hjallis Andersen broke both Olympic and world records. The actress Liv Ullmann often claims to be a Trønder – a claim to be taken as artistic licence since her place of birth was Tokyo.

The Ringve Museum of Music, outside Trondheim

Munkholmen (Monks' Island) lies off Trondheim and is easily reached (in summer) by a five-minute ferry ride. It was reputedly once used for executions; excavations have revealed what may have been an earlier church. The monastery which gave the place its name was perhaps Norway's oldest; it twice burned down and was finally abandoned in the 1530s.

The island's obvious strategic importance to Trondheim was recognized by both Frederick III, who built the still-standing bastion in 1660 (and in it incarcerated his chief minister, Count Griffenfeld), and by the Germans, with an anti-aircraft battery, in World War II.

Meeting at the church, non-orthodox

Prekestolen towers 1959 feet sheer above the Lysefjord, east of Stavanger. The small plateau that tops it – a gneiss platform some 80 feet square – is thought to have been a prehistoric place of sacrifice (and this to explain the name, which means Pulpit). Only 43 feet deep where it meets the sea near Stavanger, the Lysefjord drops to a depth of over 1300 feet below the Pulpit. Undeterred, summer sun-bathers pack the beauty-spot cheek-by-jowl, admiring scenery that Victor Hugo poetized after a visit in 1866.

Stavanger holds fourth place in the population table but can be considered 'upwardly mobile', as the 100,000 *Siddiser* (Stavangerians) are joined by recruits to the oil-fields and on-shore facilities. For this is the Oil Metropolis of the North Sea, home of the industry that has affected every Norwegian.

From the old German fighter base at Forus (and since 1989 from the modernized Sola airfield) helicopters fly almost non-stop to the ocean rigs and platforms. International airlines serve Stavanger daily – all this just north of the Hafrsfjord where King Harald Fairhair defeated his many enemies and unified Norway in 872.

The creation of Stavanger came 250 years later, when Bishop Ronald built the beautiful St Swithin's Cathedral. In 1272 both church and town burned down, but the final blow came with the Reformation, when the bishopric of Stavanger

was abolished. (It was revived in 1682 but relocated in the newly built Christiansand; the gutted cathedral was restored by Bishop Arne and endowed with its magnificent Gothic choir and altar.)

The year 1803 saw the completion of the royal residence of Ledaal, and in 1808 vast shoals of herring off the Rogaland coast brought the wealth that Stavanger had long lacked. By Alexander Kielland's time – the poet and novelist born in 1849 – Stavanger was home port for a fleet of sailing ships 300 strong. Christian Bjelland's production of brisling sardines began in 1873 and developed with other industrialists' help into a successful canning business. By then, however, the shipping fleet was obsolete, becoming less profitable, and considerable investment in new

Ledaal is the city's show-piece: a fine wooden edifice which functions both as museum and royal residence, the venue for state banquets and receptions hosted by the king or government. Erected between 1799 and 1803, it remained the property of the Kielland family until 1936, when the city assumed responsibility for it. The name is a 'reverse acronym', of not the first but the last letters of the original owners' names: Gabrie*l* Schancke Kiellan*d* and An*na* Margreth*a* Bul*l*.

industry was needed to revive local fortunes.

A theatre was built in 1883, and in 1925 the bishopric of Stavanger revived. Conditions in the 1920s and '30s were no better here than elsewhere but in 1944, and thanks to Sig. Bergesen Snr., the new Jærbanen railway brought a first taste of the prosperity to come. The shipowners Sig. Bergesen Jnr. and his brother Ole helped Stavanger to third place amongst Norway's shipping cities (second place for tankers) but, a century after the crisis of the 1880s, the industry was in grave difficulties again.

Having in 1965 incorporated the neighbouring municipalities of Madla and Hetland, the city was to benefit from having as mayor the charming Kari Thu. Both she and the late Gunn Olsen Hagen worked well in government matters.

Nearby summer beaches, with Mandal's, Norway's best

Alexander Kielland, whose family owned Ledaal for 133 years, wrote of it as 'Sandsgaard' in his novels. Born in Stavanger in 1849, he became a lawyer and industrialist but turned to writing, successfully, with *Paa Hjemveien* in 1878 and *Noveletter* in 1879. Other popular novels followed, literary fame compensating for the state's refusal to recognize his work and grant an artist's pension. This was no great loss as, first elected mayor of Stavanger, Kielland then became governor of the province of Møre and Romsdal from 1902 until his death in 1906.

Christiansand, with its 64,400 mild-mannered inhabitants, has ousted Drammen as Norway's fifth city. Chronologically it should rank far lower. For although its origins are dutifully shrouded in the mists of time (a certain Eivind, St Olav's godson, may have built a church near by in 1045), the cathedral city dates very precisely to 1641. In that year King Christian 'Quart', having just reconstructed Christiania/Oslo, set to building the *quadratur,* the 'square town' that commemorates his name. The new settlement benefitted from good anchorage well sheltered by the *skjærgård* of islands and skerries – and nowadays their beauty makes this 'capital of the south' Norway's most popular resort.

Shipbuilding, for which the city is famed, is known to have been started by 1685. (It was no doubt encouraged by the king's granting patents to 69 captains to prey on English and Swedish merchant vessels.) By 1810 Christiansand was home port to 194 registered sailing ships. (A fine example of local craftsmanship is the full-rigged wind-jammer *Sørlandet*. She came out of the P. Høivold shipyard in

1930 and still sails the seven seas.)

As with Norway's other wood-built towns, fires made progress intermittent: of a total 640 homes, 332 burned down in 1734. The hazard is still with us: after the cathedral in 1880, the Caledonian Hotel went up in flames in 1986. Both have been rebuilt.

Within a year of Christiansand's creation, by 1642, a miller was in business grinding imported grain. Industrial initiatives nowadays are Canadian Falconbridge Nickel, Elkems Fiskaa Verk, Asbjørnsens Tobaksfabrikk and the Christiansand brewery. The Royal Norwegian Air Force has based its technical training schools near the city at Kjevik, which has also an international airport. Christiansand houses the district commands of both army and navy, the southernmost bastion of the Coast Artillery being at Odderøya. Southern Norway's leading newspaper is *Fædrelandsvennen* (the Patriot), editor of which for many years was Johannes Seland, the epitome of a Christiansander.

Asked about other well-known local names, many youngsters here might mention Julius the Chimp,

star of the Christiansand Zoo (which has an unusual reputation as exporter of two-humped camels). Norway's prime minister in Stockholm in 1905, when the union with Sweden came to a unilateral end, and later president of the Storting 1913-15 was a local man, Jørgen Løvland. Two famous siblings were born here also: the poet Henrik Wergeland in 1808 and Camilla Collett in 1813. Their father Nicolai, a Lutheran minister, was a prominent member of the first Eidsvoll parliament of 1814, and later rector of Eidsvoll church. Christiansand was the birthplace, in 1871, of the novelist Vilhelm Krag, and a local wag called Tjutta, whose real name remains unknown, has a place in Christiansanders' hearts. Resistance heroes like Edvard Tallaksen and Viggo 'Viking' Axelsen live on in their grateful memory.

Drammen is not a place to which visitors often rush; its traffic in fact is such that nobody rushes anywhere much. Many Drammensers commute daily to Oslo (in first or second gear), and the place finds little favour with Norwegians generally. A pun on its name, which means 'a dram', goes: 'Just one dram (of drink) an hour is better than one hour in Drammen'.

Even the first known allusion in the archives is not wholly satisfactory. A parchment letter of 1340 describes the export of timber from the Drafn, the ancient name for the River Drammen which means murky or muddy water. On each bank developed a village, Strømsø-Kobbervikstangen and Bragernes. They received royal charters in 1636 and, from Frederick IV in 1715, the rights and privileges of merchant towns. In 1811 Frederick VI ordered their merger into the one town of Drammen. Sheltered access to the sea and the proximity of Oslo helped the unified town expand through

the 19th century, an expansion repeatedly impeded by the 'red rooster'. Drammen features in the now-familiar casualty list as: town centre burned 1850 and 1857, 206 houses gutted in 1870, 358 in 1877.

Large parts of present-day Drammen belonged earlier to the Wedel family, counts of Jarlsberg. Where Honda cars are off-loaded now and serviced, the Jarlsberg counts mined tin. If modern Drammensers differ from their fellow countrymen in their affection for the city, it is partly because of its river and the spiral road up to its plateau; to its sports clubs and athletes, and to famous sons of the city such as the philosopher-politician Niels Treschow, who sat at Eidsvoll in 1814; the composer Johan Halvorsen born here in 1864 and the author Sigurd Halvorsen in 1891.

But most local pride derives, justifiably, from Drammen's long industrial tradition. Already in the 18th century the artistic design and advanced technique of its

faience made the place famous: the cobalt mines and colour works at Modum – the Blaafarveværket that from 1759 to '73 supplied Drammen with precious cobalt pigment – have been conserved as an art institute and cultural centre. Norway's first printing press, the Mallingske Bogtrykkeri, was established in Christiania/Oslo in 1842 by the Peter Tidemand Malling born in Drammen in 1807. The Mallings, a family of merchants, had their home of Marienlyst, which is now the Drammen Museum. In 1893 the Drammen Glassworks took over from Hurdal, which had long been producing window glass prior to that. The brewery and paper-mills are important producers; a major Scandinavian paint manufacturer, Star, has its factories near by at Lier, and a total of some 30 large companies give Drammen and its 52,000 residents disproportionate industrial importance.

St Halvard's Fountain in Bragernes Tork, Drammen's market-place

Tromsø's seventh place in the population table may be debated: in 1964 the neighbouring Hillesøy, Tromsøysund and Ullsfjord were incorporated to make this Norway's largest municipality – as large as Luxembourg – and two thirds of Tromsø's 50,100 inhabitants live well out of town. If the character and attractiveness of the place and its people were our criteria, Tromsø would rank far higher.

It suffers from a tag stuck to it by a French tourist in 1900: the 'Paris of the North'. Far north it may be, but Tromsø is no Paris: there are no Gallic traffic jams for a start, and the people are far too nice. Motorists stop to let pedestrians cross not just at traffic lights and zebra crossings. Five months of sub-zero temperatures and 180 days of snow do not sit well, either, with thoughts of the Folies Bergères.

'Gateway to the Arctic' is Tromsø's more appropriate slogan. Here at 69° 20' N, the nearness of the polar regions is suddenly brought home. The Russian ships at anchor are nearer home than those from Bergen. Until 1936 no road reached Tromsø: trade and communications relied on the indefatigable *Hurtigruta*, the coastal steamers, and continued to do so until the recent development of Langnes airport. The term 'northernmost' attaches to many Tromsø institutions: the Northern Lights Planetarium and fine Tromsø Museum form part of the university, the world's most northerly. The Catholic cathedral that was built in 1861 (and in 1989 visited by Pope John Paul II) is the world's furthest north – as is its Protestant counterpart constructed the same year. The world's northernmost brewery boasts North Norway's only pub.

Tromsø takes its name from *Tromsøya* ('Troms island'), which the urban manipulation of 1964 brought within the city limits. King Håkon IV is reputed to have built a first church here, but written history begins in 1536 when a merchant on Tromsøya is recorded as trading to Bergen with small sailing vessels called *jekts* (c.f. yachts). The first Russian trading ship on record arrived in 1725, and barter trade with Russia helped Tromsø circumvent the commercial monopoly enjoyed by Trondheim and Bergen.

The monopoly was ended in 1789 and, with the northern ports free to trade on an equal footing, Tromsø became a Customs base and in 1794 acquired township status by royal charter.

With the 1820s came a new concern for seals – commercial not conservationist – and Tromsø became home port for the early arctic fleets. The whalers, too, went out from here. (Norway's last whaling station survives a short way north, catching the Minke whale, the only species not endangered.) The Bodø Museum has graphic displays of both these trades – the early whalers brave,

manoeuvring their tiny boats in heaving seas around their massive prey; the sealers unspeakable, walking amongst the defenceless herds with picks raised to club to death the waiting, wide-eyed cubs.

Opened in 1976 in a waterside Customs shed from 1789, Tromsø's Polar Museum is impressive in its tribute to the arctic explorers. The locally born skipper, Elling Carlsen, was the first to circumnavigate Spitzbergen, and from Tromsø the American Wellman set off with his curious airship on board. Having made Tromsø a port of call during his

voyages with the *Gjøa* and *Maud*, Roald Amundsen took off from here on 18 June 1928 – on his last flight to search for the lost Italian explorer, Umberto Nobile.

Through all this the northern capital was growing in stature. In 1814 it became seat of the provincial governor and – with Elverhøy Church, its oldest, consecrated in 1803 – a bishopric in 1834. Both Catholic and Lutheran cathedrals went up in 1861, the latter impressively large in wood. A municipal library followed in 1872, like the Tromsø Museum which in 1976 was merged with the university.

Victor Sparre's stained-glass window in Tromsdal Church, the 'Cathedral of the Arctic'

Tromsdal Church is the most recent and probably best known of Tromsø's places of worship. Popularly called the Arctic Cathedral, it stands unmistakable beside the beautiful Tromsøysund bridge, a white concrete triangle 115 feet high. It was designed by Jan Inge Hovig and consecrated in 1965.

The celebrated stained-glass window that forms the entire south wall was a necessary afterthought. Measuring 1507 square feet, it is claimed to be Europe's largest; Victor Sparre created it because he 'saw in Tromsdal Church a building without a soul'. The window was in fact added in 1972 to save the congregation from the stares of passers-by.

In 1812, during the British blockade of 'Napoleonic' Norway, an English frigate entered Tromsø Sound and sent out long-boats to engage two small Norwegian cutters – a naval incident eclipsed by the events of World War II. In 1940, after the Allies' withdrawal, the king and government fell back on Tromsø, which became the short-lived capital of a free Norway. From here King Haakon embarked for London when his country was forced to capitulate on 7 June 1940. Heavily invested but not damaged by the Germans, Tromsø helped to hit back in 1944. The pride of Hitler's navy, the 'unsinkable' *Tirpitz,* had been kept under observation by Norwegian agents as it steamed north and, with their help, at Kvaløy on 12 November, the battleship was attacked by the RAF and sunk. Thanks to the Høvding Shipbreaking Company, which supplied Norway's post-War foundries with thousands of tons of reinforced steel, no traces of the *Tirpitz* remain – except, that is, for the steel plates covering holes in Oslo's road-works.

Tromsø's whaling monument and the Fløyfjell cable-car

Skien is 'capital' of the southern province of Telemark. According to an old Norwegian proverb, 'a loved child has many names' – which bodes well for this town which has variously been known as Skyde, Skydeby, Skeden, Skeen and Scheen.

Endowed with a nunnery by the nobleman, Dag Eilivsson (during the reign of Sigurd 'Jerusalem' Jorsalfar), Skien has the honour of first being recorded in 1184 by Snorre Sturlasson, the writer of sagas and prime source of Norwegian history. Though gravely depleted by the Black Death, Skien was granted municipal status in 1358 by King Håkon VI – the year before he was betrothed to the six-year-old Queen Margaret.

Venstøp, Ibsen's childhood home, now part of Skien Museum

The waterfalls near which the first nunnery stood were harnessed in 1550, and the sawmills they powered had by the 1600s made Skien the kingdom's foremost timber producer. Norway's dissolution of the monasteries had put the nunnery and its properties into the hands of a local noble, Jørgen Bjelke, who in 1663 sold the sawmills to the citizens. They thrived despite fire and water: most of the town burned down in 1732 as, rebuilt, it was to do again in 1858 and 1886. In 1792 a different disaster struck: floods tore away large parts of the town and 43 vessels from their moorings.

With the Industrial Revolution, the opening of the Skien-Norsjø Canal in 1861 brought new prosperity, as did the railway to Drammen laid in 1882. Both helped open up the town to its hinterland and provide an outlet for the produce of the Telemark. The first large industry, Union Company, began business in 1873, the first power station in 1885. The urban area was enlarged in 1916, bringing the population to 16,000, and the neighbouring municipalities of Solum and Gjerpen were incorporated in 1964.

Beside the town's most famous son, the playwright and poet Henrik Ibsen, other luminaries are of lesser local interest: Captain Hjalmar Johansen who accompanied Nansen across the Greenland ice, and Gunnar Knudsen, Norway's prime minister during the Great War who, though born further south, has long worked actively for this district (in which his estate of Borgestad stands).

Skien has always been fond of sport. 'Odd' (the home team) has provided many footballers for Norway's national squad; Gjerpen supplied their handball colleagues with many first-class scorers.

Henrik Ibsen, to the Anglo-Saxon world, is as synonymous with Norway's literature as Edvard Grieg with her music and Edvard Munch with art. It was not however Ibsen who won for Norway a Nobel Prize for Literature but Bjørnstjerne Bjørnson, a contemporary far less well known (or easily pronounced) outside their native land.

Ibsen attained instead literary immortality with plays such as *Peer Gynt*, *Ghosts* and *Hedda Gabler*. Box-office acclaim and financial success, an honorary doctorate and international awards crowned a life begun in poverty and obscurity. Born in Skien on 20 March 1828, Henrik Johan Ibsen spent his boyhood on Venstøp farm after his father's bankruptcy. At fifteen he was apprenticed to a chemist in the southern coastal town of Grimstad, and at twenty moved to the capital, where he qualified in 1848 – without in any way improving his lot. With Aasmund Olavsson Vinje and P. Botten Hansen he launched a

weekly, *Andhrimner*, having a first play performed at the Christiania Theatre in 1851. After visits to Copenhagen and Dresden in 1852 he worked until 1857 as artistic director of the Bergen Theatre. In 1858 he married Suzannah Thoresen; they had one son, Sigurd (who, marrying Bjørnstjerne Bjørnson's daughter, became prime minister of Norway).

The plays Ibsen composed in this period had mainly historical themes: *Dame Inger of Austråt*, *Warriors of Helgeland* and *Royal Pretenders*. The masterpieces that won the playwright world-wide fame – *Peer Gynt*, for example, *Brand* and *Hedda Gabler*, *An Enemy of the People*, *A Doll's House* and *The Wild Duck* – were written overseas, where the Ibsens subsequently lived for many years. Invited in 1869 to attend the inauguration of the Suez Canal, they settled first in Dresden then in Rome. A generation of German writers looked to Ibsen as their mentor; he died in Oslo on 23 May 1906.

Sandnes has lately shot into the large-town league, due mainly to petroleum and the nearness of Stavanger. So near is the oil metropolis, in fact, that many think of Sandnes as its suburb. Granted municipal status only in 1965, the town has undergone a population explosion: from 32,000 in 1971 to the present 43,600. Many of these are *jærbuer*, energetic immigrants from the agricultural lowlands of Jæren.

Its raised status ended Sandnes' classification of the previous 100 years, that of *ladested* or 'trading village'. (A census of 1664 records it as a *strandsted* or 'beach settlement' with just seven residents.) A brickworks was built in 1784, and in 1868 Jonas Øglænd established the company which made his name famous and Sandnes prosperous. In later years the manufacture of

furniture became economically important to the town and surrounding district of Rogaland.

Surprisingly, the first *bedehus,* or (non-conformist) prayer-house, was not erected until 1873 – earlier at least than the state church built in 1882. The Jærbanen railway reached Sandnes in 1878.

During the War, in 1941, local government was moved to the new Town Hall and in 1959 the secondary school opened. The Rogaland police headquarters was transferred here from Stavanger in 1962, and three years later the municipalities of Høle, Høyland and Riska were incorporated. Most remarkable perhaps of the townspeople's achievements is the reclaiming of twelve acres of land from the sea.

Sandnes

Sandefjord teeters in tenth position of the population totals. With 35,839 inhabitants it beats Bodø and Ålesund by a body or two.

Nowadays the town is associated mainly with paint, as base of the Jotungruppen/Jotun A/S in which all Norway's leading manufacturers merged in 1971: Jotun-Odd Gleditsch, De-No-Fa-Lilleborg, Fleischer and Alf Bjercke A/S. But for older Norwegians Sandefjord is synonymous with whaling, not the valorous rowboat-and-spear variety but an industry that spanned the globe, earned fortunes for its magnates and made this Norway's wealthiest municipality.

Sandefjord's maritime achievements in this century are at one with its earliest history. The first mention of the site, in AD 1200, was that 'a good harbour may be found there'. That this was already well known to the Vikings is shown by the famous Gokstad Ship. The astonishing vessel now displayed at Bygdøy was excavated from a burial-mound on a Sandefjord farm in 1880. With the now-adjacent Oseberg and Tune ships, it shed a great deal of light on Viking seafaring. The six-foot skeleton it enclosed – presumed to be that of King Olav Gudrødsson Geirstadalv – has been reinterred in the original mound to which, a thousand years ago, those about to 'go viking' would come for an albeit pagan blessing.

Further mentions in the annals come in 1680, when Sandefjord became a *ladested* or trading village under the city of Tønsberg, and in 1845 when, with only 800 souls, it was granted municipal status. About that time the hot sulphur springs were harnessed and Sandefjord Bad, a curative spa, established on the spot.

Four hundred years after Columbus' supposed discovery, the harbourmaster of Christiania/Oslo, Captain Magnus Andersen, set out to prove that Vikings were first to the New World. Christian Christensen ordered from Sandefjord an exact replica of the Gokstad Ship, a 32-oar *karve*. Naming it *Viking*, Captain Andersen sailed it not only across the Atlantic but up the St Lawrence and across the Great Lakes to Chicago, where its arrival caused a sensation at the 1893 World Exhibition.

For all that, the population still in 1910 numbered only 5000, of whom 32 were to lose their lives to mines or torpedoes in World War I. The Second World War brought even higher casualties: 321 citizens died at sea with the whaling or merchant-shipping fleet or serving with the armed forces or the Resistance.

Post-War prosperity gave Sandefjord its Whaling, City and Nautical museums, then in 1958 an airport. From the fortune amassed by his mercantile empire the dying Anders Jahre donated 40 million kroner for the building of Hjertnes City Hall and cultural centre. The latter hosts concerts and is home to one of Europe's best girls' choirs, the Sandefjord Jentekor founded and led by Sverre Valen. The foundation that perpetuates Anders Jahre's name makes Sandefjord an important source of funding for scholarships and scientific projects.

Whaling, until recently, almost monopolized Sandefjord. Thousands of Vestfoldings (men of the Vestfold province) manned the fleet of huge factory-ships and smaller, faster 'hunters' built in the yards of their home port. As a full-scale industry,

Norway's whaling lasted scarcely a century. Building himself a prototype factory-ship in 1874, Gerhard Sørensen went whaling north of Finnmark. Framnes shipyard was established in 1898 to build, repair and service a whaling fleet that was by then becoming a major economic factor. With competition increasing in the Arctic Ocean, Sandefjord turned to Antarctica. A local man, Captain C. A. Larsen, made exploratory voyages to Antarctica in 1892-95 and was skipper of the *Antarctic* which accompanied the Swedish expedition led by Otto Nordenskjöld in 1901. Trade, as always, followed exploration: in 1905 (five years before

Scott and Amundsen) Christian Christensen mounted the first whaling expedition to the Antarctic Ocean. With his specially built factory-ship *Kosmos* a young lawyer, Anders Jahre, laid the foundation of the shipping, whaling and industrial empire he was later to rule from the penthouse of the Park Hotel. Lars Christensen followed in his father Christian's wake, with antarctic expeditions in 1927 and 1931. His *Norvegia*, however, had a dual scientific and geopolitical purpose: Bouvet Island and Peter I's Island were claimed for Norway, and new regions discovered and named such as Queen Maud's Land and Crown Princess Märtha's Coast.

Ålesund has, despite its name (Eel Sound), the rare distinction of being beautifully constructed in a lovely location. Over three islands of Norway's most delightful province, Møre and Romsdal, spreads a town designed strikingly in *Jugendstil*, 'Art Nouveau'. The coherent architectural style (something so lacking in Britain) resulted from a catastrophe – and from early foreign aid. In the night of 22-23 January 1904 the wooden town caught fire: winter winds fanned the flames into an inferno that left 12,000 persons homeless and became proverbial. 'Nothing so terrible since Ålesund burned down' is a Norwegian saying; locals date events as 'before' or 'after the Fire'.

Help was promptly sent by Kaiser Wilhelm II: with ship-loads of supplies and building materials came the plans for reconstruction in the then-popular German Jugendstil. For this reason Ålesund alone amongst the towns of Møre and Romsdal was not blitzed by the Nazis in 1940; a plinth and plaque still honour Kaiser Wilhelm in City Park.

Near by stands a greening bronze statue of 'Ganger Rolf, ancestor of William the Conqueror . . . presented by the town of Rouen on the occasion of the millenial (sic) festival commemorating the conquest of Normandy. Leader of the Vikings . . . was Ganger Rolf, who is supposed to have been born in the historic island of Giske by Aalesund'. If Rollo's birthplace is disputed, Ålesund's origins are certain. Recent excavations of the Borgund-Kaupangen ('trading station') site indicate a town flourishing between the years 1000 and 1500 which, with three or four churches, must have been the chief ecclesiastical centre between Bergen and Trondheim. St Olav is known to have utilized its harbour in 1028. At nearby Giske lived the Arnmødlings of whom four brothers fought alongside Olav and one led the army that defeated and killed him at Stiklestad.

Borgund-Kaupangen grew and flourished but, because of royal favour to rivals Bergen and Trondheim, lost its privileges in 1450. Only in 1793 was its right to trade restored, and full municipal status only in 1848.

Fishing more than commerce ensured the town's subsequent prosperity. '*Ålesund har sølv i bund*' is another local saying: 'Ålesund is built upon silver' – silver herring. The Sunnmøring fishermen began to reap a rich harvest from the massive shoals that came to spawn in Sunnmøre waters. In addition, *klippfisk* became significant – sun-dried cod pressed flat; as *baccalao*, this has long been a delicacy in Latin countries. The town's renewed trading status in 1793 allowed C. A. Rønneberg to establish in 1812 the successful enterprise that by the 1840s was chartering ships to lade klippfisk to Spain and South America. (Another manufacture, textiles, was started in 1849 by O. A. Devold, to become the province's largest single employer.) Another local, Nils Liaaen, began shipbuilding famously in 1861, and the introduction of marine engines brought better deep-sea fishing banks within easier reach. In 1864 Ålesund hosted a great Fish Fair, exhibiting every conceivable fish-product and requisite gear and equipment. A later innovation, the echo-sounder in 1933, enabled the fishing fleet to locate shoals and increase catches. All this, however, killed the 'golden goose': overfished by the 1950s, the herring were depleted, the catches and the fish themselves diminishing in size. Herring, for a while, had gone the way of the whale and the cod, and fishing was banned.

Whether the seals, another source of former Sunnmøre wealth, should likewise have been protected is controversial. The manner of their killing is barbaric, and a sensational film made by a fisheries inspector prompted the abolitionist activities of Brigitte Bardot, Greenpeace et al. In 1989 prime minister Brundtland bowed to international pressure and prohibited the trade. The subsequent proliferation of seals throughout Norway's northern provinces shows that this is by no means an endangered species.

Ålesund's 35,000-odd townsfolk share the Bergensers' reputation for talkativeness, and beat their southern rivals to the telephone in 1876 by ordering direct from the Philadelphia Exhibition. Recovering

from the Fire and rich from fishing and seal-hunting, Ålesund became one of the country's largest towns – and a gallant Resistance centre in the Second World War. From here Norwegian volunteers escaped the Nazi occupation; Dunkirk-like, fishing smacks and tiny boats braved the North Sea's storms to bring hundreds over to Shetland. Ålesunders served with the Allies in all the armed forces, and in such numbers that Quisling's pro-Nazi newspaper, *Fritt Folk*, printed on one front page: 'Ålesund is no Norwegian city!'.

Backed dramatically by Mount Aksla (the Shoulder), the islands of Ålesund were linked more closely to the mainland first by Vigra airport in 1958 then, splendidly, by the road tunnel completed in 1987.

Bodø is last but only historically least of the top twelve Norwegian towns. This second largest centre in northern Norway might be said to have a history in two distinct parts. What in Ålesund was 'before or after the Fire' is in Bodø before or after the bombing – the devastating air raid in the night of 27-28 May 1940 in which German Stukas flattened 420 of the town's 760 buildings. Then the coastal steamer *Prinsesse Ragnhild* sank off Bodø and a further 200 lives were lost. With 3700 homeless, the population was evacuated, mostly to the south of the country.

Compared with elsewhere in Norway, Bodø's history prior to the bombing is relatively short. (The oldest pictures in its quaint museum date from 1870 – and all appear to feature the *boghandel*, bookshop.) In the 1700s a small trading station existed here at Hundholmen, Dog Island. A century later, in 1803, some fishermen from Trondheim arrived to fish and catch whales, rendering blubber into oil. Frederick VI in 1813 decreed that the district receive a centre with municipal status but failed to say where, and it fell to the new 'independent' Storting to grant Bodø municipal rights. This in 1816 and thanks to the bishop of the northern synod, Bonsak Krogh.

The new municipality showed itself somewhat undeserving by rapidly becoming a notorious centre for smuggling. The Municipalities Act of 1837 conferred wider powers on local councils, a privilege that Bodø was unable to enjoy, having only fifteen citizens eligible to vote, insufficient to form a local council.

In 1858 the Bodø Sparebank, the first savings bank, was opened; the *Nordlandsposten*, still the town's leading newspaper, was launched in 1862. The great shoals of herring on which Ålesund was 'built' enriched Bodø also. From 1864 to 1885 they boosted the economy – and the population, which in that period increased from 500 to 2700. The Salten Steamship Company was a result in 1868. Secondary education started in 1880 and a fisheries school opened in 1892.

One year later the Hurtigruta, the indefatigable coastal express, came to Bodø and had by 1904 necessitated the construction of a new quay. In the year of Bodø's grand Industrial Fair – 1924 – the world's first factory for the artificial drying of klippfisk was built by Ragnar Schølberg. The steady development continued: a hospital and another shipping company – the Nordlandske Dampskipsselskap – in 1927, a local station of the Norwegian Broadcasting Company in 1931, and the inauguration in 1935 of a sea-plane service to Bergen, in summer only.

May 1940 brought all this to an end. Once the War was over, however, Bodø underwent a metamorphosis. The phoenix of a colourful, well-planned provincial capital arose from the ashes of the old wooden town. Even Mother Nature seemed to have taken pity, sending cod in undreamed-of quantities to the nearby Lofoten Islands. As klippfisk, stockfish or cleaned fish on ice in crates, 1,245,000 tons found ready markets overseas. Factories went up, not only for fish-products. SAS began regular flights, inheriting the fine airfield the Luftwaffe had constructed, and in 1961 the Nordlandsbanen linked Bodø to the national railway network. The Royal Norwegian Air Force has a fighter-base here, and deep inside a nearby mountain – 'somewhere in the Salten area' – the NATO headquarters for North Norway means brisk business in supplies from Bodø. Six years after the completion of the impressive City Hall in 1962, neighbouring Bodin was incorporated to give Bodø an area of 352 square miles and over 35,000 inhabitants. They have cheered their footballers, Bodø-Glimt, into the first division and have in Marianne Dahlmo one of the world's best cross-country skiers.

Nordlandsbanen, the railway north to Bodø, crossing the Arctic Circle

Tønsberg was long thought to be Norway's oldest town – until the discoveries in Ryfylke (page 31). Founded perhaps in 871, 'Tunsberg' was, under Harald Fairhair's son Bjørn Farmann ('the Merchant'), soon trading actively with the largest Viking city, Jorvik at York. Subsequent royal connections are frequent: several kings lived here, Håkon the Younger died here.

Besides several appropriately preserved vestiges of this monarchic past, Tønsberg has more recent memories of a flourishing whaling industry, and a present population of over 32,000.

Hovedøya is the site of the now-derelict monastery built outside Oslo in 1147 by Cistercian monks originally from Lincolnshire. These English and Norwegian members of Europe's then most influential order were vegetarians vowed to silence, who slept on straw and wore neither shirts nor shoes.

Halden 'guards' the Iddefjord, an eastern branch of the Oslo Fjord and Norway's south-eastern boundary with Sweden. First recorded in 1580, the town was known until 1928 as Fredrikshald in memory of Frederick III, who granted its charter in 1665. Surviving frequent fires (and recent economic set-backs), modern Halden with its 26,000 inhabitants attracts visitors most to the hilltop fortress-museum of Fredriksten.

Sellegrodfjord (left)   Halden (above)   Hovedøya (centre)

Lillehammer ('Little Hammer')
is easily reached from Oslo by
road, rail (and lake), and its access-
ibility and attractive location were
no doubt deciding factors in its
successful bid to host the Winter
Olympic Games in 1994.

Patron of the event will be no
living VIP but a 13th-century king,
Håkon IV. For it was from Lillehammer, in 1205, that two Birkebeiner
royalists escaped on skis with
Inga from Varteig's baby, to save
him from the clutches of the Bagler
faction. Raised and educated by the
Birkebeiner 'king', Inge Bårdsson,
the boy became the famous Håkon
IV Håkonsson. He founded Bergen
(Bjørgvin), dealt *primus inter pares*
with Europe's other monarchs
and even aspired to be Holy
Roman emperor; but although
immortalized in Lillehammer's
insignia, he does not appear
to have reciprocated the

gesture with fine buildings or
benefactions.

The lakeside village that sheltered the royal fugitive was at
the time called *Litlikaupangr*,
'Little trading-place' (modern
Hamar, further south, being then
Storhamar, 'Large Hammer'). Both
would have flourished as trading
and staging posts along Norway's
principal north-south thoroughfare, the Gudbrandsdal or 'Peer
Gynt's Valley'. A benign climate
favoured agriculture – convales-
cence too, with rest-homes and
sanatoriums established early.
(Another local feature of wider
renown, if smaller proportions, is
the cheese-cutter which, no doubt
prompted by the valley's fine *gjeit-
ost* or goat's cheese, one Thor
Bjørklund of Fåberg invented
earlier this century.)

Served by the main E6 highway
north, by the Oslo-Trondheim

railway and (in summer) by the
paddle-steamer *Skibladner*, the
present-day town of some 22,000
inhabitants has strong artistic and
literary connections. Lillehammer
was home to the Norwegian winner
of the Nobel Prize for Literature, the
novelist Sigrid Undset. In addition
to artists such as Thorvald Erichsen
and Lars Jorde, Jakob Weidemann,
probably the leading Norwegian
painter today, has his studio at
Ringsveen overlooking town,
lake and valley.

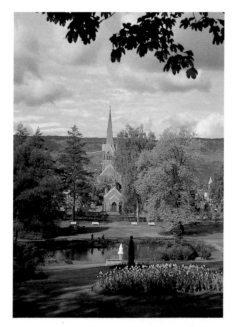

Maihaugen, of Lillehammer's several
art galleries and museums, attracts
most. Situated at the northern end of
town, it is the work of a local dentist,
Dr Anders Sandvig, who spent years
locating and assembling here the
ancient farm-buildings, complete
with tools and implements, that
now constitute this delightful
open-air museum.

The *Skibladner* is, according to the *Guinness Book of Records*, the world's oldest paddle-steamer still in service. Swedish-built and 160 feet long, she was delivered by rail – all 206 tons – and assembled on Lake Mjøsa to make a first trial run on 2 August 1856. With a new steam engine fitted in 1888, the fourteen-knot vessel helped for many years provide the key link in communications between Oslo and Lillehammer and the upper Gudbrandsdal.

Made redundant by the railway, she sank in 1937, but private and public funds and enthusiasm made possible her raising and restoration and now, a popular (if costly) pleasure steamer, the 'White Swan' plies in summer from Eidsvoll to Lillehammer, with up to 230 passengers.

Hamar, ruins of the 12th-century abbey

Autumn hunter in the Dovrefjell, the 7430-foot peak of Snøhetta in the background

The Rondane National Park covers 216 square miles of mountain astride the central provinces of Oppland and Hedmark.

103

Jotunheimen is a mountain wilderness considered by many to be Norway's most magnificent. Composed of granite-like gabbro, the region's peaks have resisted aeons of erosion and now stand, an awesome natural barrier, between the fjords of Sogn and Fjordane and the central Gudbrandsdal. Galdhøpiggen and Glittertind vie for the title of Scandinavia's highest peak: with its 8100 feet, the former is the literally firm favourite, but Glittertind is topped by a glacier which sometimes deepens and gives it winning inches. *Jotunheimen*, 'the Home of the (evil) Gods', is a name not steeped in history but given these mountains, fancifully, by one Professor Keilhau in 1822 .

Røros, quaint and picturesque for a former mining town, owes its creation in 1644 to the discovery of copper ore in the surrounding mountains. Planned and financed by the architect-king, Christian IV, the *Bergstad* ('mountain town') was taken in 1678, 1679 and 1718 by the Swedes, who destroyed it by fire on the first and last of these occasions. The fine stone church – *Bergstadens Ziir* ('Pride of the mountain town') – was built, Baroque, in 1784. The main local activity is no longer copper but tourism. Røros has been impeccably restored, the whole township now an admirable 'living museum'. The main Bergmanns Street is considered Norway's loveliest thoroughfare, and Harald Sohlberg's painting of it a treasured masterpiece.

On the practical side, there is an airport and new industry, and hotels have improved enormously since Trygve Lie first built his mountain chalet near by.

Bergmanns Street, Røros

Late 19th-century gaol on Erlia Farm, near Røros

Autumn mists over the Gudvangen valley (right)

Solo MOTELL

Traditional costumes, though frequently seen, are in Norway rarely either traditional or customary (except in the National Day parades each 17 May). The reason for this was the '400-year-long night': for most of the period 1450-1814 colourful clothing was banned by the Danish administration, which imposed grey, brown or black on all but Norwegian bureaucrats and nobles.

The practice of wearing local costume may have been prompted by plunder. In 1612, at Kringen, the men of Gudbrandsdal defeated Lieutenant-colonel Ramsay and Captain Sinclair's force of 300 Scottish mercenaries. Three hundred Scottish corpses were relieved of their kilts, and the womenfolk of Gudbrandsdal provided with cloth for their *rondastakk*

(the pattern of which should, to this day, strictly make them members of the Sinclair clan). The farmers of southern Norway who overlooked King Frederick V's debauchery and rallied to his cause, returned in 1762 from fighting his war in Holstein with what became their 'traditional dress': the short jacket and black breeches with pewter or silver buttons.

Declining with the 19th century, the use of the *bunad,* or regional costume, has increased. The beautiful version from Hardanger is the nearest thing there is to a Norwegian national dress; silver (symbolic of their rain?) predominates on what parading Bergensers wear, and Oslo's *bunad* in the city's colours – light blue, white and grey – is a recent innovation.

Hardanger fiddler and traditional *bunad* costumes

Hornadal

May blossoms in the Hardanger valley

Måbødal

Hunters overnighting in a *ljórbu*

Hardangerfjord, the 'Fjord of the Hordes', stretches 50 miles inland from the coast below Bergen to the Folgefonna glacier before branching into the Granvinfjord, the Eidfjord and the 25-mile Sørfjord (South Fjord) on which stands the industrial town of Odda.

The springtime beauty of the fruit-trees blooming lured Edvard Grieg to make his home in Hardanger, and contributes to the valley's popularity with visiting cruise-ships.

Hafslo and its lake, beside the Lustrafjord

The Sognefjell road in midsummer. This former pack-horse path reopens each June across the mountains that, once called Dølafjell, stretch from Lom in Oppland to Stryn in Sogn and Fjordane.

Geiranger is deservedly Norway's most popular fjord. It features more often than any other in posters and brochures, and nowadays seems to be automatically included in Norwegian cruises and tours. Cutting between cliffs over 5000 feet high and in places nearly sheer, this innermost arm of the Storfjord winds for some ten miles, true to its name: *Geir* means 'serpentine' (and *anger* 'fjord' – which makes 'Geirangerfjord' a pleonasm). Beauty-spots on this most beautiful of fjords are the seven Knivsflåg waterfalls (the 'Seven Sisters') and the 'Bridal Veil' at Horvedrag.

Autumn in the Meierdal

Djupvatnet Lake lies some 3300 feet above Geiranger, often remaining frozen until August and freezing again in October (below).

The Trollstig ('Trolls' steps') and its *veien* or *vegen* (road) is a seven-mile challenge, consisting of eleven hairpin bends, that delights (or frightens) visitors driving up the Trollstigheimen. Work on the road, which runs from Åndalsnes in Romsdal, commenced in 1916 but was not completed until 1936. From the savagely beautiful Isterdal (Easter Valley) the road climbs a one-in-eight gradient of 2624 feet to the 'Troll-Step Home' atop the Nuten, passing half-way the 590-foot drop of the Stigfoss waterfall.

Nigardsbreen, the glacier's 'snout' (above)

Romsdalfjord

Lofoten, meaning the Lynx's foot, also denotes the striking line of islands that rise stark from the sea, the 'Lofoten Wall', and form a 100-mile barrier between the West Fjord and the Norwegian Sea. The island-peaks are composed of granites and other volcanic rocks, gouged and scoured by glacial action in the last Ice Age. Retreating, this left a wildly magnificent terrain of almost Alpine grandeur.

The Stone Age contributed a short-lived curiosity: a dwarf horse, not a pony, that stood only four feet tall but was tough and hard-working. The species is extinct but one stuffed specimen survives in the Bergen Museum.

As for man, his story here is of little more than fishing. The Gulf Stream makes winters milder and lets grass grow lush up the steep slopes for a few flocks. But trees cannot withstand the unrelenting winds (which explain buildings battened down and heavy rocks on roofs). That the Lofotens have been inhabited for at least 2000 years is known from the remains of newly excavated farms and homes, such as at Vestvågøy. Kabelvåg is thought to be the oldest settle-ment, dating from 1120 when King Øystein decreed that *rorbuer* – fishermen's shacks – be built there. King Håkon IV ordered the men of Nordland to use the place as a base for trade, and by the 1800s Kabelvåg was the Lofotens' largest village. Neighbouring Svolvær has also mediaeval antecedents, its better harbour enabling it to surpass Kabelvåg in importance and population: now 4000 souls.

Head-counts here, however, are nullified by the annual invasion of fishing-fleets from the whole coast north and south. Their objective is the *skrei*, pelagic cod. Each year from January till late April the shoals gather on the Lofotens' shallow coastal banks to spawn. And with modern purse nets or old-fashioned longlines and handlines, the fishing-fleets would gather there too: 4-5000 boats carrying 20-30,000 fishermen (more than the entire Lofoten population) bringing in catches of up to 50,000 tons. (Before mechanization reduced the need for manpower, local fishermen were more numerous: 32,000 were officially resident in 1896.) Tonnages

Vesterålen beach

of fish caught here translate directly into kroner in the bank: Bodø owes its boom years 1864-85 to the likes of cod and haddock. It was said that a poor season in the Lofotens was felt right down to Karl Johan, Oslo's main street.

The fate of the herring, the whale and the seal has been that of cod-fish too. In the 1930s catches varied regularly between 120,000 and 150,000 tons; 1947 brought in 145,000 tons but the subsequent decline is such that the 77,000 tons caught in 1971 is spoken of as a 'freak peak'. The freezing and fish-product factories along the West Fjord now lack the wherewithal to work.

In the Second World War, and well after Norway's capitulation, the Lofotens were the scene of Allied success and failure. A first operation, on 4 March 1941, involved five destroyers, two transporters and 600 commandoes

who, at Brettesnes, Henningsvær, Stamsund and Svolvær, destroyed the herring-oil factories which produced glycerine for German munitions; took 215 Germans and fifteen Norwegian sympathizers prisoner, and brought back to Britain many welcome volunteers for Norwegian forces there.

The object of the second action was to establish at Reine a light naval base from which to harrass German sea-lanes to the Murmansk front and the convoys of Swedish iron from Narvik. Twenty-one ships landed 500 troops on Boxing Day 1941 but, informed of Luftwaffe reinforcements near by at Bodø, Admiral Hamilton ordered their withdrawal two days later. Churchill expressed himself 'disappointed over the results and critical of the decision to withdraw'.

In recent years tourists and artists have helped compensate the islands

Reine, Lofoten

for the lack of fishermen. The *ror-buer* with which King Øystein made Lofoten history now serve as simple holiday homes for visitors on a 'rorbu-vacation'. Painters attracted by the Lofoten light are becoming better known. At Svinøya, near Svolvær, an 'artists' house' has recently been constructed for six Swedish and six Norwegian painters. Local doyen is Gunnar Berg, born in Svolvær, while Kaare Espolin Johnson with his 'scraping technique' captures the mood of the islands dramatically. His Peter Dass frieze and other local themes adorn the coastal steamer *Harald Jarl*.

Farm near Eggum on Vestvågøy, Lofoten

Coastal express
North bound

Coastal express
South bound

Midnatsol, the largest and latest
steamer of the Troms Fylkes
Dampskibsselskap

Hurtigruta, the Coastal Express.

Hurtigruta means literally 'Hurried' or 'Hurrying route' (not 'hurried window', a poor local pun on the name). For generations of northern Norwegians it has meant far more: a maritime lifeline and their only all-year link with the outside world.

The accomplishment and significance of the Hurtigruta is best brought home by the map: north from Bergen to Kirkenes is the same distance as south to Milan. *2500 miles on the Coastal Steamer* is the fitting title of the excellent booklet every cruise-passenger receives. Since 2 July 1893 the trusty steamers have made that voyage day and night the whole year round.

Previously, winter communications were precarious with the three arctic provinces of Nordland, Troms and Finnmark. Though predating steam, the 19th-century coastal service was seasonal – not working in winter – and slow, not sailing by night. Improvements were impeded by the absence of charts and navigational aids, by the hazards to shipping of the arctic coast and its severe winter weather.

Superior seamanship and hard-won experience enabled Captain Richard With to overcome these obstacles, navigating day and night. Sailing the *Vesteraalen* out of Trondheim on that July Sunday in 1893, he entered Norway's history as the 'Father of the Coastal Steamer'.

The successful service With was soon operating from Stokmarknes attracted outside interest. The Bergen Line and Trondheim's Nordenfjeldske Steamship Company in 1894 became partners of his Vesteraalske Steamship Company. Together they extended the initial Trondheim-Hammerfest service: south to Bergen in 1898, north-east to Vadsø in 1907, and in 1914 on to Kirkenes.

The participating companies have varied over the years, government subsidies playing a key part in boardroom decisions. That subsidy was in 1986 guaranteed for a further ten years – three new luxury liners having been commissioned in 1982-83. Norway's northerners, once so dependent on the service, now point out with pride that all eleven *Hurtigruten* are again in northern hands.

Into the Troll Fjord, with *Peer Gynt* on the tannoy

dates it to AD 400 or thereabouts.

Like Arabia's Beduin and their camels, the Laplanders, in a very different climate, moved with their herds; they followed the grazing reindeer from the interior in winter, where lichen and moss were dug from under the snow, to the coast and islands where the spring grass grows. National boundaries and private property were of little relevance to such nomads: the whole frozen north was one vast grazing ground. However, as 20th-century 'civilization' encroached, the two ways of life collided increasingly. Confrontation in Norway came to a head with the so-called Alta Conflict of 1979: government plans for a dam and power plant on the Alta River

The Lapps, Laplanders or (as they call themselves) Sami are found throughout arctic and sub-arctic Europe – from the Kola Peninsula in Russia to Dalarna in Swedish Lappland and Norway's province of Finnmark. Of the estimated total of 35,000 Lapps, 22,000 live in Norway.

Other than the self-evident fact of their being nomads of Mongolian origin who speak Saarme (a language akin to Finnish), little is known of Sami history. Norway's Komsa Culture of 6000 BC is considered Lappish by some; others accept finds 4000 years younger as the first sign of Lapp life here. Unquestioned evidence of settlement – such as at Kjelmøy near Kirkenes –

were opposed by Laplanders fearful for their herds.

Modern techniques (and local diplomacy) pre-empt such problems today. New methods of butchering and packaging, sometimes by mobile units on the spot, have reduced to a minority the number of Lapps now engaged in reindeer-herding. Despite contamination after Chernobyl, the increasing popularity (and price) of reindeer-meat has improved the Lapps' standard of living. Their two towns of Karasjok and Kautokeino have been provided with amenities such as cinemas and church, and in 1989 the Lapps were granted their own parliament, or *Sameting*, with Professor Ole Magga as first

parliamentary president. The first session was inaugurated by King Olav, who spoke of his rôle as equally King of the Lapps: widespread and well-calculated media coverage brought the Lapps into the limelight of 20th-century life.

Reindeer and sled-trek across the Finnmarksvidda

Sautso, Europe's largest canyon

The midnight sun, seen here at the North Cape, is a remarkable phenomenon that those who have not seen it may find hard to envisage. Observed above a certain latitude (which is not precisely but just south of the Polar Circle), the sun simply does not set for several months. Nor, conversely, does it rise in winter.

The cause is naturally the earth's tilting, and dates are determined by the latitude. At 67° 20' N the sun shines day and night on Bodø from 5 June to 9 July; on Tromsø, at 69° 20' N, from 21 May to 23 July. Seen from the North Cape, the sun remains above the horizon from 12 May to 1 August (and remains invisible, in unbroken night, from 19 November to 25 January).

As Norway's, and Europe's, northernmost point, the Nordkapp/North Cape attracts some 100,000 visitors each year. Chambers cut inside its sheer 1000-foot cliff house a restaurant, a post office for the obligatory viewcards franked 'North Cape', a cinema and a tunnel of dioramas, the last donated in 1989 by rotarians from Thailand to commemorate the visit in 1907 of their King Chulalonkorn (he of *The King and I*).

Spitsbergen, the name of Norway's largest arctic island, has been generalized to cover all her Arctic Ocean territories, which Norwegians themselves call Svalbard.

Stretching between latitudes 74° and 80° N, the islands are administered but not owned by Norway. They were first mentioned in 1194, in Icelandic records which read simply '*Svalbardi funnin*', 'Svalbard is found'. The name of Spitsbergen ('Pointed peaks') came with the Dutch explorer Willem Barents, who rediscovered the islands in 1596 but failed to elicit any colonizing response from his government. His English contemporary, Henry Hudson, followed in 1607 and his reports of the potential for trapping, sealing and whaling soon prompted expeditions from England, France, Germany and the twin kingdoms of Denmark and Norway. In the last, King Christian IV opined that the islands belonged historically to Greenland, and thus to him, but had no means of implementing his claim. The need to determine sovereignty diminished with the territory's commercial returns: over-hunted for some 250 years, the islands supplied less and less.

The discovery of coal gave national borders new importance in the 1900s. Most commercial activity on Spitzbergen, first in furs then in coal, had been Russian; but in 1920, the signatories of the Svalbard Treaty in Paris awarded sovereignty to Norway, not Russia. Enforcing it de facto only with effect from 14 August 1925, Norway governs through a *sysselmann*, a senior civil servant from usually the Ministry of Justice.

All partners in the Svalbard Treaty reserved themselves equal mineral rights but only Norway and Russia exercise them, and both only with coal. The Russian community is centred on the mining town of Barentsburg; base for the 1000-odd Norwegian miners is Longyearbyen, 'Long-year Town'.

They enjoy, thanks to the Gulf Stream, a climate remarkably mild for so northern a latitude. The environment is none the less hostile, and stark: gouged by ice and glaciers, Spitzbergen's arctic peaks rise over 5000 feet.

Diminutive Spitsbergen reindeer (centre)　　　　Svalbard walrus

Longyearbyen, Spitsbergen

Magdalenafjord glacier, Spitsbergen

Index